Understanding Housing Finance

Understanding Housing Finance offers a distinctive introduction to the subject. Instead of discussing housing finance in accounting or economic terms, this book considers housing finance *politically*. It is finance that makes housing consumption, housing management and housing development possible, but in order to understand housing finance we need to appreciate the workings and principles that are at the heart of current policies.

Understanding Housing Finance covers the development of housing finance by concentrating on the main political mechanisms. The book develops two core themes. The first is the manner in which central government aims to regulate housing through control over financial structures. The key to understanding housing finance is this political control. Governments, be they Conservative or Labour, have felt the need to extend and maintain political control over housing and it is this that makes finance so important.

The second theme is the shift towards personal subsidies. The book looks at the development of housing subsidies and mechanisms in all tenures and shows the increasing importance of subsidies to individuals, instead of subsidies to build new dwellings. The political approach also aims to show the links between the main tenures and the importance of unintended consequences in the development of policy.

Understanding Housing Finance is an accessible and up-to-date introduction for those beginning their studies and will be a useful reference for more advanced students. There are clear learning objectives and summaries in each chapter, as well as annotated further reading. Learning activities are highlighted throughout the text and are designed to assist the reader in developing issues or for reflection on important principles. A full glossary is also provided.

Peter King is Reader in Housing and Social Philosophy in the Centre for Comparative Housing Research at De Montfort University, Leicester. He is the author of *Housing, Individuals and the State: The Morality of Government Intervention* (Routledge, 1998) and *Housing: Who Decides?* (with Michael Oxley, Macmillan, 2000).

Understanding Housing Finance

Peter King

London and New York

First published 2001
by Routledge
11 New Fetter Lane, London EC4P 4EE

Simultaneously published in the USA and Canada
by Routledge
29 West 35th Street, New York NY 10001

Routledge is an imprint of the Taylor & Francis Group

Typeset in Times by Keystroke, Jacaranda Lodge, Wolverhampton
Printed and bound in Great Britain by Biddles Ltd, Guildford and King's Lynn

British Library Cataloguing in Publication Data
A catalogue record for this book is available from the British Library

Library of Congress Cataloging in Publication Data
King, Peter, 1960–
    Understanding housing finance / Peter King.
        p. cm.
    Includes bibliographical references and index.
    1. Housing—Finance—Government policy—Great Britain. 2. Housing subsidies—Great
Britain. 3. Housing authorities—Great Britain. 4. Housing policy—Great Britain.
    I. Title.

HD7333.A4 K56 2001
363.5′82′0941—dc21   2001019494

ISBN 0–415–23547–2 (hbk)
ISBN 0–415–23548–0 (pbk)

 # Contents

 **Tables**

 # Preface

Housing finance is fun! At least, that is what I have spent the past ten years trying to convince my students. The reality is, of course, that for most students housing finance is something to be got over. Most will probably admit that it is for their own good to know where the money comes from and why there is never enough. Yet one can't help feeling that they would rather leave it to someone else to find out for them.

In recognition of this reluctance, I've thought long and hard about ways of making housing finance enjoyable. I've tried several different approaches and methods. In desperation I've even contemplated using a glove puppet, but then glove puppets have still got to find something interesting to say! Perhaps the best thing, then, would be to get someone else to teach it (which is exactly what somebody else thought at De Montfort University in 1993).

What I resort to now is the expedient of suggesting that at some time in the future, not now or even next year, but sometime, I will be thanked for forcing this medicine down their throats. Indeed, one or two of the several hundreds I have taught housing finance to have come up to me and said as much. And to such things do desperate people hold on.

The way I have developed my housing finance teaching is to remove almost totally any accounting notions and, most important of all, any numbers from the syllabus. My courses are truly housing finance for the innumerate (in my case a necessity). But there is some serious intent in this. There has been a tendency to become engrossed in specific technical issues and mechanisms. This is valid, but what is lost is an overall view of where housing finance policy fits into the world around it. This book aims to offer the big picture and to place housing finance into broader processes. It doesn't deal with the full complexity of housing finance, and indeed there are a number of issues I have neglected or ignored altogether. It certainly doesn't deal with financial management and accountancy. This is not because they are irrelevant or unimportant, but rather because I have something else to say that I consider more important and which has not been said in this way before (and in any case, I decided if I couldn't please everybody, I should at least please myself).

What I have tried to develop is a *political* approach to housing finance, which looks at the principles and processes that operate within housing policy. This book is the result of this development and is the result of honing my thoughts on housing finance systems and processes for nearly ten years. I justify my particular approach in the first chapter, but I would say that this approach has developed out of my own desire to understand housing finance more fully.

Another reason for concentrating on broad themes is that it is impossible to stay absolutely up to date in housing finance. Policies have changed and developed considerably in the year and a half I have taken to write this book. I am sure that things will have changed between sending the manuscript off and its being published. Hence what I have tried to do is concentrate on principles and processes, showing the continuities and the points where many changes have occurred. The aim has been to ensure that after reading this book, one will be able to see *why* things have changed.

The book is aimed primarily at students. I have tried to make it as accessible as possible so that it can be read even by those with a limited understanding of housing issues. But also I hope that the discussion will be of interest to a more advanced readership.

Each chapter contains a number of learning activities relating to the text. These can be used in a number of ways. Readers can see the learning activities as natural breaks allowing time to reflect, reinforce or extend the concepts discussed in that chapter. But some of the learning activities might be used as assignments or classroom activities. Some of the assignments would take only a few minutes, whilst others would take an hour or two. Suggested answers are included as an appendix at the back of the book.

I have also included a glossary of key terms at the end of the book. In it I have tried to give simple and straightforward definitions of mechanisms and concepts that are important for the argument for this book.

I have a number of people to thank for their help and support whilst I was writing this book. First, I owe a great debt to those anonymous reviewers who have assessed and commented on the book at various stages from synopsis to final draft. The book has been improved considerably in terms of clarity and rigour as a result of their wise words. I am also grateful to Andrew Mould and Ann Michael at Routledge for their support, advice and assistance. I am fortunate to have a number of colleagues within the Centre for Comparative Housing Research at De Montfort University who have offered advice and constructive criticism on parts of the book. In particular, Deborah Bennett, who also teaches housing finance at De Montfort University, has acted as both a sounding board and an exacting critic for my ideas on housing finance. I have also benefited from many discussions with Tim Brown on housing finance and housing policy more generally. I must also thank the very many students who have been so good as to turn up week after week in the vain hope of being inspired (let alone being amused). Finally, I must thank those closest to me – Barbara, Helen and Rachel – for their forbearance, support and, above all, their patience. On with the fun.

1 ▶ Understanding housing finance

- ● What housing finance is
- ● Where it comes from
- ● Why housing finance is needed and, particularly, the issues of quality and access
- ● The political approach to studying housing finance

Introduction

Housing finance is all too often seen as a dry technical subject which we all realise we ought to know something about, but would rather ignore. We assume we have to be numerate and understand accounting principles. We might also be frightened of the jargon and the heavy use of acronyms such as HIPs, HRAs, RSF, PWLB[1] and so on. Indeed, having taught housing finance for ten years now, and at various levels, I am aware that fear is one of the main stumbling blocks to understanding housing finance. Students and housing practitioners put themselves off by assuming that housing finance is too complex and difficult for them to comprehend. Not surprisingly, their fears are frequently confirmed. Most people, I would suggest, have an attitude problem when it comes to housing finance.

However, this book aims to take a different approach to the subject with the aim of taking some of the fear away. Instead of concentrating on numbers and accounts, the book will discuss housing finance as primarily a *political* issue. My aim is not only to discuss how the current systems of housing finance operate, but also to look at their political function. I want to analyse why they operate as they do and how they came about. This means a combination of history and policy analysis along with the more straightforward description of housing systems.

---

1 A glossary of terms is provided at the end of this book.

It also means a concentration on the discussion of issues, rather than bombarding the reader with endless statistical tables and graphs. I firmly believe that it is important that one understands the underlying and enduring principles behind housing finance and not be too worried about exact amounts spent here or there. Those data can be picked up easily from government websites and from public documents. What is less readily accessible is what significance these figures might have. One can gauge the importance of particular housing finance data only when one understands the principles behind them. This doesn't mean that I will ignore the numbers entirely, rather that I will use them only when they back up the argument. The figures quickly go out of date, but the underlying principles have remained the same for the past twenty years. Therefore, if one understands the principles, the rest will fall into place.

But also an understanding of housing finance is necessary if we are to properly comprehend other aspects of housing. Housing management is little more than paper policies unless we have money to employ staff. Housing development is just plans unless we have the finance to build and renovate. We need to appreciate the role of housing subsidies in encouraging and controlling the activities of landlords. We need to understand how a lack of income can affect the housing of many households. Furthermore, we need to appreciate the effect of rents and mortgages on household budgets. Little or nothing can be done about housing without money. Therefore to understand housing, we have to understand housing finance.

In this chapter I wish to explore why housing finance is important. I shall begin by defining what I mean by housing finance. From this I shall suggest that the two most important issues in housing finance are quality and affordability. It is how these two issues interact that creates the dynamics within housing finance systems. I shall consider what finance is needed for and where it comes from. Finally, I shall consider the merits of a political approach to housing finance in more detail.

What do we mean by 'housing finance'?

Put simply, housing finance is what allows for the production and consumption of housing. It refers to the money we use to build and maintain the nation's housing stock. But it also refers to the money we need to pay for it, in the form of rents, mortgage loans and repayments.

There is a tendency to think that housing finance is all about subsidies and therefore about credit approvals, housing revenue account (HRA) subsidy, social housing grant, housing benefit and mortgage interest tax relief. These are all important, or have been, and we shall indeed spend large parts of this book considering the various forms of government subsidy. However, we need to be aware that there is more to housing finance than subsidies.

The majority of British households are owner occupiers who pay for their housing from their own income. Therefore much of housing finance is found privately, mainly from earned income. Of course, a household's income is normally used to repay a loan provided from a commercial bank or building society. This is another important source of housing finance. In addition, households use their own money and borrow in order to fund repairs and improvements to their dwellings. They also spend money on decoration, furnishings and fittings.

Private finance has also become increasingly important in the social rented sector. Since 1989, housing associations have used private finance alongside government subsidy to develop new social rented housing. The possible introduction of arm's-length companies and the increased use of stock transfer and the Private Finance Initiative also indicate an increasing reliance on private finance in the local authority sector.

So we need to be aware that housing finance consists of more than subsidies from government. It involves the far larger sums spent by households and housing organisations that are derived from income and from borrowing. But there are two further facets of housing finance we need to consider.

First, housing is a store of wealth, and thus we need to be aware of the fact that the housing stock is an asset that can be used by its owners. Individuals can and do tap into this wealth in order, say, to set up a small business, pay school and university fees for their children or enjoy their retirement. Landlords can use their assets as security for future development. Thus housing wealth can allow households and landlords to develop housing and non-housing activities.

The second issue returns us to the role of government. Because housing is so expensive and so valuable an asset – as well as being so important to our well-being – government feels the need to regulate housing finance. It can do this through interest rates that affect mortgage repayments, and by controlling rents through rent controls and regulating standards which impose and limit costs on landlords and tenants. Therefore we need to consider not just the money that government spends on housing, but the costs that its actions impose on the various players involved in the production and consumption of housing.

A consideration of what housing finance is also tells us where the money comes from. It shows us that, whilst some finance comes from government, we need also to consider other sources such as earned income and private finance. Table 1.1 summarises what I take housing finance to include.

Table 1.1 *What housing finance is and where it comes from*

- Government subsidies to landlords and households

- Households' own income used to provide, maintain and improve their housing and the amenities within it

- Private finance from mortgage lenders and financial institutions to fund house purchase and social housing development

- The wealth stored in housing which is used to fund housing and non-housing activities

- Government regulation of housing which imposes or limits costs, such as building regulations and rent controls

Why do we need housing finance?

Table 1.1 also begins to tell us why we might need housing finance. I would suggest that we need it for at least four reasons:

- to build new dwellings;
- to cover a household's housing costs in the form of rent or mortgage repayments;
- to fund necessary maintenance and improvements to dwellings; and
- to manage the housing stock to ensure it meets certain political and social objectives, such as fulfilling urgent housing need.

Without finance we could not achieve any of these objectives.

But this offers only a partial answer to the question of why we need finance, in that it does not explain why government has a role. We need to appreciate this because government does not intervene in the same manner with all households. The list of facets that housing finance covers shown in Table 1.1 does not apply equally to all households. In particular, government's role differs according to households' income and therefore their ability to provide housing for themselves. In some cases government offers financial support and regulation, whilst in others (and this is the majority) it merely regulates standards. Moreover, this regulation might directly or indirectly impose costs on households, rather than providing them with financial support.

All this suggests that housing finance fulfils a more specific purpose over and above the general objectives described above. I would suggest that this purpose is to ensure a housing system that offers quality and access to all households.

Quality and access

Housing is one of the most important items that we human beings need. There are many things that we would find difficult, if not impossible, to do without good-quality housing. We might find it hard to find and keep a job, to learn, to maintain our health, to vote, to claim benefits we are entitled to and to initiate and maintain stable relationships.

But just because something is important, this does not mean it is always available. Like most commodities, housing comes with a price tag attached. If we want decent housing we have to pay for it. It also follows, broadly speaking, that the better the standard of housing we want, the more it will cost us. Therefore, as standards rise, so does the cost.

One of the most important issues, then, is how we can afford the sort of housing that we want. We could say that this is simply a case of matching up our income with our aspirations and expectations and buying the best dwelling we can afford. This may be fine for those on reasonable incomes, but not for those on low incomes. Many households will lack a sufficient income to provide them with a dwelling that meets their expectations. It may well be that they could find housing of some sort, but this might not be of a standard that they, or the society of which they are a part, find acceptable.

This implies that two issues are of supreme importance. The first is *quality*. We are not content with just any type of housing; we want good-quality housing that allows us to live a civilised and healthy existence. We therefore require housing to a modern standard of amenity. This standard, of course, is a relative one, in that it depends on general expectations that exist here and now. It is no good saying that households elsewhere in the world manage with less or that our grandparents were brought up without central heating and modern appliances.

The second issue follows on from this, and is about *access*. We might readily agree on what constitutes a good-quality dwelling for us here and now. We can describe the particular amenities and standards that the modern dwelling should have. But that doesn't mean that everybody has such a dwelling. Many households might not be able to afford one.

There is a clear trade-off between quality and access, in that, generally speaking, the higher the quality, the fewer will be able to gain access to it. Quality comes at a cost, and this limits access. There is, then, a gap that needs to be filled, between the aspirations people have for good-quality housing and their ability to access it because of a lack of income. This is where housing finance comes in, by acting as the bridge over this gap.

Therefore the true purpose of housing finance – and the historical reason why the state has intervened to provide subsidies – is to ensure that all citizens gain access to good-quality housing. Put simply, *housing finance exists to make quality housing affordable.*

A political approach to housing finance

Having defined what housing finance is, I now wish to define the approach I intend to take in studying it. My approach is, I believe, distinctive from that of other housing finance texts. Most tend to rely on economic analysis to understand housing finance (Gibb *et al.*, 1999; Hills, 1991; McCrone and Stephens, 1995; Oxley and Smith, 1996). Others rely on policy studies to inform their analysis (Malpass *et al.*, 1993). Instead of these approaches I shall rely on a *political approach*.

My aim is to stress the wider political processes that affect housing policy. Studies reliant on economics or policy studies can offer and have offered valuable insights into housing finance, but they have their limitations. In particular, they tend to underplay the wider context in which housing organisations operate.

My aims in this book are to show that:

- Housing systems operate within dynamic open systems. This means that factors external to housing systems (inflation, unemployment, poverty, etc.) impact on housing, and thus problems cannot be solved by purely internal processes. Housing problems can often be solved only by using non-housing solutions.
- The impact and effect of unintended consequences on policy outcomes are considerable. Because of the complexity of housing systems, not all eventualities can be predicted or taken into account. This places a severe limitation on the policy process itself. The most destabilising issues in politics are those that have not been foreseen. Housing is not immune from these events and we need to be aware that they will happen, even though we can never predict what they will be and when they will occur. Many of the most important housing phenomena, such as the decline of private renting and large-scale voluntary transfer, were not foreseen.
- Individual households have a considerable impact on housing outcomes, and thus we need to go beyond the study of institutions and structural forces. We have to be aware of the impact of issues such as need and choice and how the behaviour of households and landlords meshes into policy.

I believe one can model housing systems to show three distinct levels that have different, if overlapping, functions. These three levels are identified in Table 1.2.

Table 1.2 *Three levels of housing politics*

Level	Agents
Planning	Central government
Implementation	Social and private landlords, mortgage lenders, professionals
Personal	Households

Of course, Table 1.2 is a considerable simplification of the housing process. The three levels are not independent of each other, but are related. Moreover, these relationships are unpredictable, not only because each level affects the others, but because many external factors also influence the outcomes at each level.

But by holding onto this model we can understand the political relationships that operate within housing and gain a fuller appreciation of how systems work. It recognises some extremely important facets of the housing system that we need to appreciate:

- Planning and implementation take place at different levels and are undertaken by different organisations. Governments make policy, but it is implemented by other organisations at another level. Hence there is the possibility of political conflict, divergence of interest, and misunderstanding and misinterpretation. It is important to realise that there is not necessarily a shared interest across all three levels.
- Housing is experienced at the personal level, and the process therefore does not stop at the implementation level. We need to understand the impact at the personal level, and it is primarily (though not exclusively) at this level that we can measure success or failure.
- Because there are three distinct levels, there can be a multiplicity of external factors that impact on the housing process. Moreover, because the three levels are functionally interrelated, an external influence at one level can influence behaviour at the other levels. An example of this is the impact of unemployment at the personal level and the consequences this might have for the policy and implementation levels (see the discussion in Chapter 5 of the recession in owner occupation in the United Kingdom in the early 1990s).
- This implies that concentrating only on one level will give us a misleading view on how the housing process operates. We would never be able to explain housing phenomena satisfactorily by concentrating on just one level.
- But because we cannot predict the influences or pre-empt the effect of the various interrelationships, we can never fully appreciate the housing system in all its complexity, apart from by hindsight.

The model shown in Table 1.2 is therefore a simplification of what is an extremely complex set of relationships, and one that may well be immune to a complete understanding. However, this does not mean that we should not try to understand more than we currently do. Indeed, it is only by appreciating and accepting our limitations that we can make any progress at all.

Understanding housing finance

This book, then, offers a political understanding of housing finance. What this means is that we cannot even attempt to understand housing finance without three things:

- We need an appreciation of history. We need to understand how we have got where we are now. This is partly because we cannot wish away our present circumstances, but also because we need to see if there are any patterns that will help us predict the future.
- We need to understand how all the parts of the housing system fit together. We need to appreciate that the growth in certain tenures has been at the expense of others and that some households are helped from the income of others.
- We should understand that politics involves the exercising of expectations and aspirations as well as economic resources. Tenants and owner occupiers are also voters, parents, homebuilders and citizens. What is more, they carry out these roles concurrently and without seeking prior permission from government, landlord or mortgage lender. They are also likely to see these roles as more important than whom they are a tenant of or whom they make their mortgage payments to. Regardless of tenure and ownership, a dwelling is always somebody's home.

Somewhat perversely, therefore, a political appreciation of housing finance indicates that we need to consider more than just money!

It is my belief that in order to understand housing finance one needs to appreciate certain principles and trends that have been influential for a significant period of time. Housing finance changes with a bewildering frequency. This means that any housing finance text is out of date almost before it is published. However, most of these changes follow a pattern that is dictated by the past. Of course, we can never predict what will happen in the future. However, we might be able to understand what has happened because we appreciate the principles and themes that have dominated housing finance over time.

In this book I aim to consider these principles and trends. Thus, even if systems and policies have changed (and they will have), the changes will be understandable because of how they relate to the patterns of the past.

Centralised control

The main theme of this book is that housing policy has become increasingly centralised over the past twenty-five years. Any notion of local autonomy has been eroded by governments, which have become more concerned with controlling public expenditure than fulfilling local housing needs. Accordingly, central government has developed ever more sophisticated mechanisms for controlling housing providers to ensure they meet the government's priorities.

Much of the discussion in the chapters that follow will be framed by this notion that central government attempts to control housing activity. The only way to understand housing finance over the past three decades is by looking at how government has tried to control the activities of organisations at the implementation level. Thus central government dictates rent levels, sets performance indicators for service delivery and uses subsidy to ensure its aims are met.

Yet this does not mean that central government always achieves its aims. The fact that new and more sophisticated mechanisms are frequently needed implies that government is never able to control housing for very long before unforeseen circumstances and events intervene. Housing is always provided locally and always enjoyed privately. This places limitations on what government can understand about housing processes. If it doesn't have a full understanding, it is unlikely to be able to control housing systems effectively.

But even though control is by no means absolute, it does have the effect of stifling local differences. The ability of local organisations to respond to genuinely local issues is hampered by the need to meet national priorities and because one is judged by national standards.

Thus the key to understanding housing finance is *political control*. It is the need to extend and maintain political control that makes finance so important, for it is through financial mechanisms that political control can be exercised.

The scope of this book

This book is not intended to be comprehensive, although I hope that the key areas have been well covered. In adopting a political approach to housing finance I have left out any discussion of accounting principles and I have dealt with economic principles only where this is unavoidable. These approaches are covered elsewhere, whilst a political approach is not. Therefore there has been a price to pay in adopting a distinctive approach to housing finance, but I hope that this is worth it for the insights gained by this approach. Inevitably the topics chosen for discussion, and the manner in which they are discussed, reflect my interests and may hint at my political orientation. I hope, however, that I have covered the main issues.

There is, though, another area in which this book is not comprehensive, and that is the differences that exist between housing finance in England on the one hand and Scotland and Wales on the other. My expertise (such as it is) is in English housing finance and I have, somewhat reluctantly, decided to concentrate largely on what I am confident in dealing with. On a more substantive level, there is a political reason for concentrating on English housing finance rather than dealing with all of Britain. Devolution since 1997 has meant the political separation of many areas of social policy. Increasingly the political control of housing in Scotland and Wales will become distinct from that in England as the devolved government and assembly bed in and develop. Therefore, increasingly the Scottish and Welsh systems will become distinct and separate from the English system. I would argue in partial mitigation, though, that much of the discussion in this book is equally applicable to Scotland and Wales.

A final point I wish to make is with regard to style. I have deliberately limited the use of graphs and tables in this book, believing that discussion is a more satisfactory approach. Those tables I have used help to illustrate trends and principles and as such they are embedded in the mainstream of the discussion. My aim has been to attain a readable, yet discursive style. One of my main concerns about other housing finance texts is that they are full of tables and graphs, without adequate explanation. My experience is that readers can make more use of clear exposition than a list of numbers.

Summary

In this chapter I have:

- defined housing finance;
- considered why we need housing finance;
- suggested that quality and access are the key issues;
- considered what a political approach to housing finance consists of;
- introduced centralised control as a key theme in housing finance; and
- outlined the scope of this book.

Further reading

There are a number of other housing finance textbooks, which whilst taking a different approach are all useful in their way. Gibb *et al.* (1999) offer a largely economic analysis of housing finance, whilst Garnett (2000) mixes economic analysis and accounting principles. This latter text is very detailed and puts housing organisations into their broader financial contexts. Malpass and Aughton (1999) have provided what is intended as a basic guide but is very straightforward and readable. These books, whilst dealing with the same subject matter, are quite different from this text. A detailed, if rather advanced critique of approaches to housing finance can be found in King (1997).

In terms of a political approach to housing finance, my book *Housing, Individuals and the State* (King, 1998) explicitly takes this approach, without being as comprehensive as this book in its coverage of housing finance issues. See also King and Oxley (2000) for a debate between the political and the economic approaches to housing.

2 ▶ The state, the market and subsidies

- The nature of state intervention in housing
- The roles of the state and the market in housing provision and consumption
- What subsidies are and how they are used by government

Introduction

In this chapter I wish to explore the roles of both the state and markets in the provision and consumption of housing. This will lead into a discussion of why housing, for some people if not for all, has been subsidised. As we discussed in Chapter 1, housing finance involves private activity on the part of households: saving, borrowing and paying rent. Yet it is also about government providing funding for particular groups, on the basis of need (as in social housing) or for other, more political, purposes (as in the case of owner occupation) and through regulatory mechanisms which set standards and ensure performance. Government and private initiative can be seen as complementary – the 2000 green paper talks about government aiding people to fulfil their aspirations (DETR, 2000a) – but the state and the market can also be seen as antagonistic. This was the case in much of the rhetoric of the Conservative governments between 1979 and 1997, which argued that state provision, such as council housing, stifled choice and individual responsibility, whilst these virtues were fostered by owner occupation (DoE, 1987).

This chapter explores the relationship between the state and the market and concentrates on two issues:

- whether, in the light of the Third Way politics of the Blair government, such a dichotomy is still relevant; and
- what subsidies are and how they can be used.

The aim is to establish some of the key issues and concepts that are crucial to understanding housing finance. The next chapter considers how subsidies have developed by looking at the history of housing over the past hundred years. These two chapters should be seen as complementary and reliant on each other, in that one discusses the purposes of subsidies (this chapter) whilst the other (Chapter 3) looks at whether these purposes were fulfilled and why the situation arose in the first place.

The state or the market?

One could suggest that government action is necessary because of the failings of markets to provide good-quality, affordable housing for all. The history of housing finance, which I consider in the following chapter, can be seen as the story of how government has become more involved in housing provision. Yet, on the other hand, most households in the UK purchase their dwelling through a market. In this sense markets clearly work.

Much of the debate in housing finance, at least when it is looked at politically, can be seen in terms of the basic opposition between state and market provision. It is therefore useful to begin a consideration of the role of housing subsidies by looking at this basic dichotomy between the state and the market. This is important because state intervention is frequently justified on the basis of the failings of markets, whilst state provision is often compared unfavourably to market provision.

The state can be seen as a political community organised territorially. Hence we talk of the British state. It is where political power is located and exercised within a particular country. The state can be defined as *a compulsory political association which successfully claims the monopoly of physical force within a given territory*. Thus the state has the power to make political decisions and ensure that they are implemented, if necessary by force (MacCormick, 1993).

The state is often conceived of as an acting subject, in that it is considered to be a body in itself that acts, and we say that the state does this or that. However, the state really acts through a series of individuals and organisations functioning as the organs or representatives of the state. These bodies are very extensive, and in Britain include the following:

- central government including the Prime Minister, the Cabinet, government departments, the civil service and, now, the devolved governments in Scotland and Wales;
- semi-autonomous bodies such as the Housing Corporation or the Arts Council that have been established and funded by Parliament, usually to fund private organisations;
- Parliament, made up of the House of Commons and House of Lords, but also now including the Scottish Parliament and the Welsh Assembly;
- the law courts, judges and magistrates, etc.;
- the armed forces;
- the police;
- local government; and
- the Church of England and the Church of Scotland as the respective established churches.

All these bodies act on behalf of the state, fulfilling different functions at different times. In terms of housing, the organisations acting on behalf of the state are central government (the British and Scottish Parliaments and Welsh Assembly), semi-autonomous bodies such as the Housing Corporation, the law courts in enforcing and interpreting law, and local government. The last of these owns and manages housing as well as playing a role in the enforcement of standards.

Like the state, the market can be seen as an entity, but it too is really a set of relations. But most markets do not exist as physical entities. The market is merely a way of describing 'a set of transactions by which money and goods change hands' (Levine, 1995, p. 48). As Levine states, a market can refer to all transactions – hence we can speak of national and even global markets – or the name can be applied to a specific subset of all transactions, such as the labour market or the housing market. These subsets can be further subdivided, so that we can talk of local housing markets, the private rented market and the owner-occupied market.

Levine (1995) helps us to understand how the state and markets are distinct by looking at how they relate to wants and needs. Wants are things 'we choose for ourselves as a way of expressing who we are' (pp. 31–2). The most appropriate vehicle through which to exercise choice and self-expression is the market. A want is something desirable and we may consider it necessary, but it is usually something we can live without.

By contrast, needs are things 'imposed upon me independently of my will' (ibid., p. 31). One can have a need even when one is unaware of it. We may need a major operation, but be unable to interpret the symptoms ourselves. Needs also often have a greater imperative attached to them, in that they are immediate and have serious consequences if neglected, e.g. serious illness, starvation. Thus it is often argued that certain needs should be provided at the point of immediate need regardless of ability to pay. This means that somebody other than us should ensure that these needs are met, which implies a co-ordinating function that goes beyond the market – the market operates only when we choose to buy or sell. This co-ordinating role has been taken up by the state.

Thus to concentrate on needs leads us to contemplate government action, whilst a concern for wants is more likely to leave us satisfied with markets. Thus those with severe housing need, caused by a lack of income, disability, discrimination or whatever, should be able to rely on the state to fulfil their need. But those who have a sufficient income are able to exercise their choice in the housing market.

Therefore the state and the market can be portrayed as having different functions. Of course, the situation is no means as clear-cut as this basic dichotomy between wants and needs might suggest. Markets, in practice, are regulated and it is government that is the regulator. Likewise, governments, both Conservative and Labour, have tried to introduce so-called 'market disciplines' into the provision and management of social housing. Thus we have planning and building regulations and laws aimed at protecting individuals from the mis-selling of mortgages and gazumping. But also we have Compulsory Competitive Tendering, Best Value and the use of private finance in housing association development. Markets and the state are therefore closely intertwined. Does it therefore make any sense to talk of the state and the market as opposites?

I would suggest that whilst such a division is by no means clear, it might be worth persisting with for at least two reasons. First, the terms 'state' and 'market' are important politically. They carry with them some political baggage, which might help us to associate with or against particular perspectives. An enhanced role for the state has been associated with the left and parties such as Labour, whilst the market is more associated with right-wing politics and parties such as the Conservatives. But this does not mean that the right sees no role for the state, or the left totally rejects markets. Conservatives, for instance, see a clear role for the state, but it might be limited to that of protecting individual property rights and thus to supporting markets. It is perhaps more accurate to suggest that the debate is frequently about 'how much state' and 'how much market'.

Second, seeing the distinction between the state and the market in these terms helps to show in which direction policy is moving. If we are looking towards market solutions to housing problems, this clearly implies a reduction in the role of the state. Again, this ought not to be seen in absolute terms, but rather is relative to what has gone before. Therefore the terms 'state' and 'market' can be seen as shorthand for particular directions in policy-making.

But one could respond to this argument with the rejoinder that housing policy, like many aspects of public policy since 1997, is attempting to go beyond simplistic right–left or state–market splits. We have, apparently, a government seeking to steer a Third Way between the traditional dichotomies of politics (Brown, 1999b). The Prime Minister at the time of writing, Tony Blair, makes this distinction himself when he defines the Third Way as 'a modernised social democracy' (Blair, 1998, p. 1). For him this represents 'a popular politics reconciling themes which in the past have wrongly been regarded as antagonistic' (ibid.). He goes on:

> Liberals asserted the primacy of individual liberty in the market economy; social democrats promoted social justice with the state as its main agent. There is no necessary conflict between the two, accepting as we now do that state power is one means to achieve our goals, but not the only one and emphatically not an end in itself.
>
> (ibid.)

The Third Way is therefore seen as a means of reconciling the state and the market into a new politics that takes the best from each side.

Wood and Harvey (1999) discuss the financial aspects of this Third Way in housing and show that it consists of initiatives such as the Private Finance Initiative, where the private sector, driven by profit, becomes involved in social housing. What the Third Way seeks to achieve, be it in housing or more generally, is to develop a partnership between the public and private sectors which draws on the best elements of both sectors. Thus the aim of Third Way thinking is to cast the dichotomy between the state and the market into the dustbin of history as a redundant relic of failed policies of the 1970s and 1980s.

But regardless of the labels which politicians may wish to put on their policies, one is still talking about the mix of state and markets.

Privatisation in the 1980s was about shifting the balance from state to private ownership. Compulsory Competitive Tendering was about market-testing public services to improve their efficiency. Likewise, the Private Finance Initiative is just a further attempt to introduce private-sector disciplines into public services. What we are still dealing with, despite the rhetoric of the Third Way, is the continuation of the dialogue between state and market. The Blair government is not really charting a course between these two 'extremes', but is aiming for a particular mix, and this is precisely what has occurred under previous governments.

The 'baggage' which the terms 'state' and 'market' carry with them is important and informative. These terms help to portray what has been, and still is, a significant political divide. They allow us to see the direction of policy and to picture the debate in which housing finance sits. Housing finance is a tool that allows government and individual households to achieve their desired aims. Housing finance can be public and private and it can fuel both state and market activity. In trying to determine the political uses of housing finance this dichotomy will remain useful.

ACTIVITY 2.1

Consider why the state intervenes in housing markets. What are the main ways in which it intervenes?

What are subsidies?

One of the main ways in which the state intervenes in housing markets is by providing subsidies to landlords and households. This might be to make housing more affordable, to encourage landlords to build more or better-quality housing or to ensure that the housing stock is of a sufficiently high quality. We therefore need to understand what role subsidies play. This will allow a fuller understanding of the role of the state. But it will also inform us of the qualities and failings of housing markets that have caused the government to intervene.

A starting point is to try to define exactly what subsidies are. In simple terms, subsidies are intended to make housing cheaper and more affordable than it otherwise would be. A more technical definition is offered by Oxley and Smith (1996), who define a housing subsidy as 'an explicit or implicit flow of funds initiated by government activity which reduces the relative cost of housing production or consumption below what it otherwise would have been' (pp. 40–1). This is a useful definition for several reasons. First, it suggests that subsidies can be used for all housing tenures. Whilst there is a tendency to concentrate on social housing, we need to be aware that governments also subsidise the private sector, through housing benefit and improvement grants, and owner occupiers through a variety of tax reliefs and tax exemptions. Second, this definition does not just refer to the use of public funds. The reference to an implicit flow of funds can be seen as a reference to measures such as rent control, which saw private landlords effectively subsidising their tenants. Third, it covers all types of subsidies from tax relief to owner occupiers to government grants to housing associations and is therefore a tenure-neutral definition. It also demonstrates that subsidies can be directed towards landlords to assist them in building, managing and maintaining dwellings, but also to the consumers of housing in the form of tax relief or income supplements such as housing benefit.

The debate about what subsidies are is also very much tied up with how they are used. For instance, many politicians have refused to see tax relief to owner occupiers as a subsidy, even though this has arguably had a much greater impact than, say, subsidies to housing associations. Likewise, subsidies paid to housing organisations, which allow them to build new dwellings at subsidised rents and to maintain their existing stock, have a purpose *and effect* on housing systems markedly different from those of subsidies paid to individuals to assist them in affording market rents. Subsidies to housing organisations assume we need more housing, and are therefore explicitly aimed at increasing the supply of housing. Subsidies paid to individuals will not necessarily encourage an increase in the supply of housing, but are rather intended to help households afford what already exists. Therefore, to fully understand what subsidies are, we need to look at how they are used.

ACTIVITY 2.2

List those housing subsidies that either you have received or you currently do receive.

What is the purpose of subsidies?

So subsidies aim to make housing more affordable. However, within this larger aim, government might seek to achieve other aims. We therefore need to look at the purpose of subsidies in more detail. As we shall see in more detail in Chapter 3, housing subsidies were introduced soon after the First World War. The aim was to deal with a shortage of good-quality housing which all households could afford. Therefore the main purpose of subsidies between 1919 and 1976 was to deal with this shortage by encouraging local councils (and, latterly, housing associations) to build new housing and to regenerate existing dwellings to bring them up to modern standards of amenity.

But subsidies can also be used to encourage particular forms of activity. For example, in the 1950s government encouraged slum clearance, but then in the 1970s the policy changed to one of rehabilitation. Accordingly, the type of subsidy offered was tailored to meet these changed policy objectives. Another important example of how subsidies can direct action followed the Housing Subsidies Act 1956. This Act gave £22 annually per dwelling to build traditional houses, but £66 annually per dwelling for flats of fifteen storeys and above (Power, 1987). The effect was to encourage high-rise development even though high-rise blocks were more expensive to build and maintain, and proved to be less popular than traditional housing.

It is important to realise therefore that government subsidies can be used to direct the activities of local housing providers. But subsidies also have a further purpose, namely to control the activity of housing organisations. Subsidies can be used as financial leverage, to force housing organisations to operate in a manner amenable to central government's aims. Over the past twenty years the purpose of subsidies has moved away from the relatively straightforward notion of *subsidy as support* to that of *subsidy as control*. Thus measures such as deficit housing subsidies, HIPs, notional housing revenue accounts and restrictions on the use of capital receipts can all be seen as attempts to control local authorities to ensure they fulfil the wider aims of government. Thus the primary, but implicit, aim of housing subsidy is now to control activity rather than to encourage it.

This leads on to the second issue with regard to the purpose of subsidies, which relates to how and to whom they are distributed. In 1976 over two-thirds of subsidy was paid out in the form of bricks and mortar, or *object* subsidies. These were aimed at allowing local authorities and housing associations to provide new additional housing at subsidised rents. It was felt that the best way to deal with the housing shortage was to offer financial incentives to encourage social landlords to build dwellings. The main effect of these subsidies therefore was to increase the *supply* of housing.

The remaining third of housing expenditure was paid out in the form of tax relief to owner occupiers and rent rebates. Subsidies of this kind are referred to as *subject* or *personal* subsidies. Their aim is to make housing more affordable by increasing household income. They therefore have the effect of increasing the *demand* for housing.

However, this balance between object and subject subsidies has now been almost totally reversed, with over 78 per cent of subsidies now in the form of subject subsidies (Wilcox, 1999). Throughout the 1980s and into the early 1990s, mortgage interest tax relief (MITR) to owner occupiers had increased dramatically from £2.2 billion in 1980/1 to a peak of £7.7 billion in 1990/1 (Wilcox, 2000). Since then MITR has declined and was completely phased out in April 2000. But since the late 1980s housing benefit has increased and more than replaced the cost of MITR to the Treasury. In 1988/9 the total cost of housing benefit was just over £4 billion, but by 1998/9 the figure had climbed to £12.5 billion (ibid.). At the same time, gross revenue and capital subsidies to local authorities and housing associations had fallen from £6.6 billion in 1988/9 to £3.2 billion in 1997/8 (ibid.). Indeed, as we shall see in Chapter 4, central government has actually been making a net surplus on local authority housing revenue accounts since 1994/5. Table 2.1 outlines the change in subsidies between 1980 and 1997.

Table 2.1 *Changes in housing subsidies, 1980–97*

	1980/81		1990/91		1996/7	
Housing benefit	£0.4bn		£5.7bn		£12.2bn	
MITR	£2.2bn		£7.7bn		£2.4bn	
Sub-total	£2.6bn	(43%)	£13.4bn	(70.1%)	£14.6bn	(75.6%)
Gross social housing investment	£4bn	(57%)	£5.7bn	(29.9%)	£4.8bn	(24.4%)
Total	£6.6bn		£19.1bn		£19.4bn	

Source: Wilcox (2000)

Kemp (1997) suggests that this general shift away from object subsidies occurred for three reasons. First, the end of massive housing shortages meant that a reassessment of the housing problem was needed. The problem was now seen as one of a shortage of income rather than a shortage of housing. Second, Kemp points to the perceived 'fiscal crisis' of the welfare state in the 1970s and 1980s. This essentially was the belief that the welfare state was unaffordable in its current form. The economic problems experienced by Britain, like other countries, in the 1970s meant we could no longer support the burgeoning cost of welfare. Third, he suggests that there was a general belief in market solutions to problems in social and public policy, leading to an emphasis on the importance of the consumer over the producer of services.

This change in the balance between object and subject subsidies implies a change in the purpose of housing subsidies. Instead of subsidy being used to increase supply, it is now aimed at bolstering demand. The belief is that there is enough housing for the number of households in the country. What is therefore at issue is not the quantity of housing, but whether all households can gain access to housing of sufficient quality. It is therefore the issues of *access* and *quality* that are at the centre of the shift from object to subject subsidies.

However, despite this shift in subsidy, the majority of academic commentators on housing finance still argue that object subsidies are a more effective way of subsidising housing. Therefore the shift in the balance of subsidies over the past twenty years is a controversial one (see Barlow and Duncan, 1994; Hills, 1991; and King, 1998 for fuller discussion of this debate). Many organisations, such as Shelter, continue to argue for the need for more investment in new social housing. Other commentators, such as Smith (1997), demonstrate that Britain lags behind other West European countries in terms of housing investment. It is worthwhile therefore to look at the purported advantages and disadvantages of the two forms of subsidy. In many ways one can see that the advantages of one form of subsidy also indicate the perceived faults in the other form. Thus listing the advantages of object subsidies can inform of the pitfalls of subject subsidies and vice versa.

ACTIVITY 2.3

What are the effects on housing organisations of the shift from object to subject subsidies? Who has benefited from this shift?

Arguments for object subsidies

The first argument is that housing is a merit good and it is therefore socially desirable to provide good-quality housing. Merit goods can be defined as 'goods which society believes individuals should have but which some individuals decide not to purchase' (Oxley and Smith, 1996, p. 11). They go on to relate this to housing provision by suggesting that '[g]ood quality housing can be viewed as a merit good which will bring benefits to individuals over and above those which individuals perceive' (ibid.) and that '[t]here is a case for governments encouraging the provision of merit goods which will inevitably be under-provided in a market system' (ibid.). Merit goods are therefore goods that individuals ought to consume at a certain level, because it is good for them. However, they may not be fully aware of this benefit, or may choose not to consume to the desired level. Thus there might be a discrepancy between what individuals wish to do and what society as a whole thinks is best. Therefore subsidising the supply of housing can ensure a greater level of provision than if it were left to individuals. Note that according to this argument, there still might be a problem even if individuals had the money to provide for themselves.

The second argument in favour of object subsidies is that housing consumption is politically acceptable, whereas a cash payment, which could be used to purchase such things as alcohol and tobacco, might not be. As a society we approve of certain activities as being legitimate for subsidy, but not others. Thus we should ensure that public money is spent on things which benefit individuals and not merely on wants and desires.

Third, it is argued that poor-quality housing can lead to problems such as ill health, vandalism, racism, family break-up, etc. If people live in poor-quality housing they may become ill, or if there is a shortage of suitable housing in an area it might stir up racial tensions, if some groups believe they are being excluded and others given preferential treatment. The point is that housing can have far-reaching effects that go beyond fulfilling the wants of individual households. Housing provision, or the lack of it, can have social effects and it is difficult for individuals to deal with these problems themselves. However, building more social housing and to a high standard can help to deal with these social problems.

A further problem is that because of the differences in land and property values across the country, there are differential costs in a rental market that can be ironed out by object subsidies. Subsidising the production of social housing, even if it means paying higher levels of subsidy to landlords in high-cost areas, means that rents can be similar across the country. This can encourage labour mobility as well as being seen to be fair and just. Another example of this form of subsidy is the Starter Home Initiative announced in the 2000 green paper (DETR, 2000a). This initiative aims to use subsidies to assist key workers such as nurses and teachers to afford housing in expensive high-demand areas.

Fifth, it can be argued that benefit take-up will be below 100 per cent and thus some people may miss out on what they are entitled to. This might be because they are unaware of their entitlements, or because they perceive a stigma attached to handouts from the state. Thus it might be best to fund housing providers to ensure that good-quality housing is available without the need to claim benefits.

Another problem with subject subsidies is that they can create a poverty or employment trap because individuals are reluctant to take low-paid work because of the way in which their benefits are withdrawn. For instance, under current housing benefit regulations 65 pence of benefit is withdrawn for every extra pound a claimant earns. When one takes into account the increasing tax and national insurance paid as earnings increase, one can see how one might be better off on benefit. But providing the goods 'in kind', in the form of social housing, would help to deal with this problem (assuming, of course, that rents were not too high).

As we have seen, object subsidies can allow for greater control over the quality of housing enjoyed by low-income households. But they can also ensure that recipients do not benefit excessively from public funds. One problem with subject subsidy systems is that they can lead to the phenomenon of demand creation or 'up marketing'. This is where individuals rent a larger and more expensive property than they strictly need. But, because their rent is paid for them, they have no incentive to economise. The system of local reference rents for private rented housing was introduced in 1996 with the specific aim of controlling this problem.

We should also remember that social landlords need capital subsidies not merely to build new dwellings, but to maintain and improve the existing stock. Whilst they could find this money from rental income, it might be more efficient to fund major repairs through subsidies and thus place less of a burden on rents.

Lastly, and perhaps most importantly, object subsidies act as direct incentives to supply new housing. If one has a shortage of housing, as has been the case in most Western countries throughout the past century, subsidising landlords is the most direct and effective way of getting houses built. But it also encourages quality by allowing landlords to build to a higher standard than they might if left to a market where they would perhaps be more concerned with covering their costs and making a profit.

There are, then, a number of strong arguments for the use of object subsidies. However, as we have seen, there has been a shift away from this type of support and a move instead towards subject subsidies aimed at helping individual households afford access to housing. We therefore need to look at the advantages of subject subsidies and, along the way, plot the possible disadvantages of object subsidies.

Arguments for subject subsidies

One of the main justifications for subject subsidies is that they can be targeted to those in need and can be withdrawn when the beneficiaries' income increases. Households allocated a council house can stay there all their lives, regardless of how their income and personal circumstances change. Thus needy low-income households might be denied access to social housing because more affluent households remain in occupation, even though they might now be able to afford owner occupation or private renting. This problem has been further compounded by the effect of the right to buy, which has allowed these more affluent households to purchase their council house and thus permanently reduce the stock of available dwellings. A system of subject subsidies, however, would prevent this because households would be subsidised according to their current circumstances and not their past. The subsidy could thus be withdrawn if and when their circumstances changed.

Second, subject subsidies can offer, in principle at least, households some choice over where they live and the type of accommodation they wish to reside in. If the subsidy is paid directly to the household, they are able to exercise more control over their lives than if the subsidy was paid to landlords who built where and what they felt was required. Of course, in Britain much of the housing benefit paid out goes directly to the landlord, and this detracts from that particular advantage of subject subsidies. But this is not a necessary part of the system and could be remedied by a change in policy (King, 1999, 2000).

This relates to the third point, namely that it could be argued that object subsidies give too dominant a role to landlords at the expense of tenants. Landlords are able to exercise control over rents and the level of service offered to tenants. However, paying the subsidies to the tenants would give them some negotiating strength over rent levels. It would create a different and more equal relationship between landlord and tenant.

A further advantage given for subject subsidies is that they can be tenure neutral, in that they can be applied to all housing sectors, including owner occupation. Where subsidies are in the form of personal income payments they can allow ready access to all tenures. However, this is not a feature of the British housing benefit system, which operates differently according to tenure (see Chapter 8).

In discussing object subsidies the issue of stigma arose, and I suggested that this might be a reason for preferring subsidies to landlords instead of handouts to tenants. But this is an argument that can be turned around and used against object subsidies. Whilst in the past there might have been a stigma attached to welfare benefits, this has now diminished and has been replaced by a stigma attached to social housing. The stigma is not attached to welfare, as now so many more receive it, so much as to whether one is a council tenant. Owner occupation is now so much the dominant tenure that there is perceived to be a fault with those who haven't achieved it and must rely on state-provided housing. It could be argued that this stigma could be avoided by individual payments allowing households to purchase or rent privately.

Whilst object subsidies are said to help landlords build good-quality housing, there is no automatic link between this form of subsidy and quality outputs. Local authorities and housing associations have been guilty of building poor-quality and unpopular housing (Page, 1993; Power, 1987, 1993). As we have seen, local authorities were encouraged by the subsidy system in the 1950s and 1960s to build high-rise blocks, which are not universally popular and, as with the example of Ronan Point in 1968, have proved on occasion to be disastrous.

Moreover, it is argued that object subsidies have led to ghettoisation and unbalanced communities (Marsland, 1996). They have created large estates where many of the occupants are economically inactive and where those who can afford to leave do so. However, it is only fair to say here that the majority of households in social housing are in receipt of welfare benefits and therefore it might actually be the effect of subject subsidies that has created this situation.

This last point shows the dangers in polarising this debate on types of subsidy. Whilst one can paint a picture of two systems in opposition to each other, it is important to remember that in Britain we have a mixture of the two systems. We have a situation where object subsidies still go to social landlords, but with a comprehensive housing benefit system also supporting tenants. Social landlords still receive revenue and capital subsidies to help them to build new stock (in the case of housing associations and other registered social landlords) and manage, maintain and renovate their existing stock. But also the majority of social housing tenants receive housing benefit to help them pay their rent. Indeed, as we shall see in Chapters 4 and 5, social landlords have become increasingly reliant on housing benefit as a relatively secure form of subsidy.

We thus have a hybrid subsidy system and there appears to be no real prospect of object subsidies disappearing totally as has occurred, for instance, in Australia and New Zealand (Kemp, 1997). What is clear, however, is that there has been a considerable shift towards subject subsidies. This is based on the premise that households should have more choice over where they live and be responsible for their own income, rather than relying on landlords to take all the decisions for them.

A final point one could make is that the two forms of subsidy have different functions and thus might be appropriate only in certain circumstances. Thus it might be the case that object subsidies are particularly useful in dealing with chronic housing shortages and when there is a need to change things fast. Thus object subsidies were necessary in the past when Britain needed to build millions of dwellings. But now that that shortage has passed and we have a crude surplus of dwellings, we should focus more on ensuring that households have access to good-quality dwellings. Also, because there is no longer a crude shortage, we are able to put more emphasis on choice.

ACTIVITY 2.4

Discuss why in Britain we maintain elements of both object and subject subsidies.

Summary

In this chapter I have:

● looked at the role of the state and the market in the context of housing policy;

- suggested that the dichotomy between the state and the market is a valid political distinction;

- defined housing subsidies in such a way as to include all forms of support and all tenures; and

- considered the purpose of housing subsidies and made the distinction between object and subject subsidies.

Further reading

For more discussion on the nature of housing subsidies, see Barlow and Duncan (1994) and Hills (1991), who each offer comprehensive defences of object subsidies, and King (1998) for a position favouring subject subsidies. Oxley and Smith (1996) also give a clear overview of the issues.

3 The development of housing subsidies

- The key issues in the development of housing subsidies
- The increasing role of government in the development of housing systems
- The effect of unintended consequences on the development of housing systems
- The piecemeal nature of this development

Introduction

In order to understand current systems we need to appreciate how we got them. What have been the reasons why housing finance systems have developed in the way they have? Is it part of a long-term strategy by governments, or have today's policies and institutions arisen out of a series of accidents? Table 3.1 shows that the changes in the structure of housing provision have been considerable, with a long-term decline in private renting, owner occupation becoming the dominant tenure and local authority housing growing and then declining.

My aim in this chapter is to show that the development of current provision has arisen out of a combination of both accident and design. Successive governments have followed housing policies aimed at increasing both the quantity and the quality of housing. But many

Table 3.1 *Changes in housing tenure (England and Wales) (%)*

	1914	1951	1971	2000
Owner-occ.	10	31	50	69
Private rent	89	52	19	11
Local authorities	1	17	29	15
Housing associations[a]	—	—	—	5

Sources: DETR (2000a); Malpass and Murie (1999); Wilcox (2000)

Note: [a] No separate data were collected on housing associations until the 1981 census.

developments have arisen not out of deliberate policy, but despite it. What the following discussion continually highlights is the effect of unintended consequences, and how government quite often is unable to predict outcomes with any accuracy or immediacy. This does not mean that government has no effect. Its effects, as we shall see, are all too obvious. However, government may not achieve what was intended.

What this historical study also shows, though, is that we have moved from a market-dominated housing system with only light government regulation, to one dominated by government activity and the desire by the centre to control the activity of housing providers. Yet a look at the history of housing shows how selective that intervention has been. We have moved from a situation where, at the start of the twentieth century, most households provided for themselves through the rented housing market, to a situation where a majority provide for themselves through the owner-occupied market. This reinforces the point made in the previous chapter that the discussion on the state and markets is not a simple either/or, but a complex relationship. A brief historical overview will assist in understanding this complex relationship further.

The nineteenth century

The development of subsidies has its roots in the nineteenth century. The reasons leading to government intervention are complex and we cannot do them full justice here. We can rather merely look at the broad trends.

The nineteenth century saw a large and unplanned influx of people from rural to urban areas. This was due in the main to technological changes in agriculture, which reduced the need for labour, at the same time as industrialisation and the development of urban centres were taking place. This shift in population had two effects: an increase in the demand for housing leading to an increase in rents, and overcrowding of existing housing. This overcrowding, allied to poor conditions, increased the susceptibility to plagues such as cholera. Whilst infections might have started in poor areas, plague was no respecter of class boundaries and thus the effects of overcrowding were felt across the urban population.

For this reason, early housing legislation such as the Public Health Act 1848 placed an emphasis on sanitation rather than overcrowding or dealing with low income. Thus legislation that affected housing in the nineteenth century was aimed at improving public health and the

perceived causes of infection. The result was an emphasis on clearing
unfit housing, but without any obligation to replace this stock. Of course,
this was also a period when, because there was no comprehensive form
of income maintenance, insecurity of employment led to large numbers of
households with an intermittent income or no income at all.

Housing in relation to public health was seen as a local problem even in
the early nineteenth century, and thus issues of sanitation were the
responsibility of the local parishes and city corporations. Indeed, poor
relief had been a parish responsibility since the mid-seventeenth century.
Whilst this local connection is important for the later development of
housing provision, it was also one of the major reasons for the lack of any
action to remedy poor housing conditions until after the First World War.

Until the electoral reforms of 1867 and 1888, voting and electoral office
were linked to property ownership. One could vote because one owned
property of a certain type and value. Moreover, one paid local rates on the
basis of one's property. It was the conjunction of these two elements that
helped to maintain poor housing conditions and shortages in urban areas
throughout the century. Local property owners, who were renting out
lodgings to the poor, were given the responsibility to regulate, yet they
would be the very ones asked to fund the cost of new building or
improvements. In consequence, a number of Public Health and Dwellings
Acts passed between 1848 and 1909 were largely ineffective, because
they gave local councils and corporations powers to improve housing in
their area, but didn't make them duties. Thus the ethic of non-intervention
in individual property rights was reinforced by the interests of electors
and elected alike.

This does not mean, however, that there were no calls for greater
government intervention in housing. Indeed, following a Royal
Commission on vagrancy and poor housing in London, the Housing
of the Working Classes Act 1890 did give local authorities the power
to construct working-class dwellings. However, as Daunton (1987) has
suggested, many local authorities felt that these powers were
'inappropriate'. Moreover, central government provided no money
to assist in any building projects.

There was, however, some charitable activity in the second half of the
nineteenth century. Several of what are now large housing associations
such as the Guinness Trust, Peabody Trust and the William Sutton Trust
were endowed by rich benefactors to provide dwellings for the urban
poor. Others from the 1840s onwards were determined to show that

'dwellings for the labouring classes' could be developed and managed at a profit. This movement, which became known as 5 per cent philanthropy because of the intended rate of return, built so-called model dwellings aiming to show that such schemes were feasible. However, rents were not within the reach of the poorest, and this approach did not become the 'model' for future development (Malpass and Murie, 1999).

The First World War and after

So, even though attempts had been made to improve housing provision, and some had been calling for government intervention since the 1880s (Daunton, 1987), the turning point for government intervention in housing came with the First World War and its effects on local housing markets. The war had the effect of creating huge shifts in the population as a large number of active males went abroad to fight, leaving gaps in the labour force at the same time as there was an increased need for industrial labour to provide war *matériel*. There was therefore a further influx from rural to urban areas. The need to prioritise production for the war effort, however, meant that there was a shortage of building materials, which in turn meant that there was no new building during the period of the war.

As had occurred periodically throughout the nineteenth century, 1915 saw a significant increase in rents in many large cities, due to a combination of increased demand and the impossibility of increasing supply. This situation led to rent strikes in key industrial areas, such as Glasgow, that were crucial to the war effort. In response, the government introduced the Increase of Rent and Mortgage Interest (War Restrictions) Act 1915, which fixed rents and interest rates on mortgages at their August 1914 levels. This Act had the effect of defusing rent levels as a crisis issue and, as an emergency measure, it was intended to be repealed once the war ended. On one level, therefore, the Act was a success. But it can also be seen as assisting in the devastation of private renting as the dominant housing tenure. In 1915, 89 per cent of households were in private rented housing, whilst the figure is now 11 per cent.

The Act had the effect of imposing rent ceiling for most rented housing, and this can be seen as the first attempt to subsidise housing. As with all subsidies, the aim of rent control was to make housing cheaper, something achieved in this case by making it illegal for landlords to increase their rents. Thus, over time, rents became lower than they would otherwise have been.

However, whilst rent control was a subsidy, it did not operate in the same way as those now used by government such as housing benefit and social housing grant. Although government insisted on the measure, it did not itself fund the subsidies to tenants. This cost fell on landlords, who were unable to increase rents, and thus their income, even when their expenditure had increased.

This Act was significant for two reasons. First, it was important because it was the first time government had actively intervened in property rights in a proscriptive (rather than permissive) manner to try to manage housing provision and consumption. Second, it also showed quite early that government action will always have unintended consequences, because once the Act was in place it became politically difficult to repeal it. The housing shortage merely worsened at the end of the war in 1919 as men on war service returned, and there was relatively high inflation in the early 1920s. Whilst this Act was subsequently amended and partially repealed in 1923 and 1933, it was not fully removed until the 1950s. The intention of rent controls was the entirely laudable one of protecting tenants, but the net effect was to contribute to the long-term decline in the private rented sector. Landlords were unable to increase their income in line with increases in expenditure and thus found it harder to improve and maintain their properties. As a result, many landlords took the opportunity to leave the market and invest their capital elsewhere.

But there was also a further reason for the decline in private renting. It quickly became clear that rent controls were not sufficient to deal with the post-war housing problems. Rent controls did nothing to deal with vagrancy and poor conditions. Indeed, by reducing supply, they merely made them worse. Government, as many on the left had been urging since the 1880s, began to look to more direct methods both to increase the total housing stock and to improve its quality. This involved the first attempt at direct government subsidy in the so-called Addison Act of 1919. This introduced Exchequer subsidies to local authorities, which would cover the liability on any debts incurred above a penny rate contribution. This was a generous system, and the resulting houses were of good quality.

In 1923 this subsidy was altered to a fixed subsidy whereby a local authority received £X per dwelling for Y years. This formula for subsidy remained intact right up until 1972, with only the level of X and Y altering when government tried either to encourage more development or to reduce expenditure.

Thus central government began to subsidise local authorities to build and manage council housing. What is significant, however, is that subsidies were not in the form of grants to fund development, but were to help a local authority repay loans it had taken out in order to build. Local authorities had to borrow to fund their housebuilding programmes and government committed itself to subsidise the capital and interest payments. This remained the case right up until 2001, with subsidy being used to offset debt liabilities.

The inter-war period also saw an increase in owner occupation, particularly in the 1930s, which was a period of rising real incomes, static house prices, and the development of building societies as sources of secure and stable investment which maintained a high degree of liquidity. The result was a boom in owner occupation fuelled by competition amongst building societies flush with funds. Thus the fastest-growing sector in the inter-war years was not local authorities but owner occupation. Indeed, the boom in owner occupation in the 1930s occurred during a period when subsidies to local authorities were substantially cut (Boddy, 1992).

A further significant development occurred in the Housing Act 1935, which required local authorities to operate a *housing revenue account* and permitted *rent pooling*. These appear merely to be technical accounting changes, but the effect was considerable. The creation of housing revenue accounts (HRAs) was important in that it made local authorities account separately for their housing function and led in time to the creation of separate housing departments. But of crucial importance was the ability of local authorities to rent-pool. This means that they could combine their income and expenditure on all their housing stock into one account, whereas previously they had to account

---

ACTIVITY 3.1

List the benefits to tenants of government intervention into housing. Why was intervention resisted by landlords?

---

separately for projects built under different legislation. Local authorities no longer had to tie rents to production costs, but could relate them to amenity and attributes. This has made the production of new dwellings considerably cheaper in that rents on existing stock can be used to hold down those of newly built stock.

Despite these developments, the most serious issue in the late 1930s was still that of a shortage of good-quality housing. This problem was only compounded by the effects of the German bombing of some major British cities and a virtual complete end to new building during the Second World War. The immediate priority for the post-war Labour government elected in 1945 was to deal with this accumulated shortage of dwellings.

After the Second World War

The issues facing government in the immediate post-war period were a chronic shortage of housing caused by war damage and an inability to build, compounded by an increase in demand created by an increase in household formation and a baby boom. The priority therefore in 1945 was to start building housing as quickly as possible.

The twenty-five years following the Second World War was a period of massive expansion of council housing, largely due to the increase in subsidies in the Housing Acts of 1946 and 1952. Much of the impetus for this increase came through the election of Clement Attlee's Labour government in 1945. However, despite some attempt to reduce subsidy and decontrol rents in the late 1950s, the Conservatives followed a similar policy of building council houses. Council house building never fell below 150,000 per annum throughout the 1950s and remained in excess of 80,000 right through to the end of the 1970s. One can therefore suggest that there existed a considerable consensus around the issue of dealing with a shortage of dwellings, namely that it should be met by mass council building.

But, as we discussed in Chapter 2, government subsidy can be used to influence the type of housing as well as the overall numbers. This can be seen by the Housing Repairs and Rents Act 1954, which encouraged slum clearance and private sector improvement, whilst the Housing Act 1956 offered higher subsidies for high-rise building. Thus government used the subsidy system to encourage local authorities to build certain types of dwellings.

There are two significant points to be made here. First, governments have attempted to direct local authorities (and, more recently, housing associations) through targeted subsidies. Thus social landlords are not left to determine their own priorities, but have them dictated to them by central government. Second, one merely has to look at the aftermath of the 1956 Act, with its encouragement of high-rise housing, to see that the effects of housing finance are long term. Housing is a long-lived asset, and whilst this means that it can provide a long-term benefit, the liabilities hang around for a considerable period too.

The 1960s was a period of consolidation, but also one of steadily improving rights and protection for tenants. It saw an increase in council house production, particularly after the election of a Labour government in 1964.

The 1970s and the end of consensus

The 1970s, however, saw the beginning of some quite fundamental changes, which are still being felt now. The period saw major changes in the operation of housing subsidies. This came about largely for two reasons. First, the economic problems that became manifest in the 1970s, with the economy being plagued by high inflation and increasing unemployment simultaneously, led to cuts in the public housebuilding programme and the attempt by both the Heath and the Callaghan governments to impose greater controls. Thus the 1970s is important because it saw a change in emphasis away from the encouragement of council house building and towards the limitation of development to match government public spending targets.

The first signal of this change in policy came as early as 1972 when Edward Heath's Conservative government introduced radical reforms of housing finance, changing the capital funding system which had operated since 1923. The Housing Finance Act 1972 made three important changes, all of which have had lasting effects. It ended the discretion local authorities had traditionally enjoyed over rent-setting by extending the 'fair rent' system already in operation in the private sector. The aim of this policy was to increase rents considerably, allowing for subsidy to be reduced. Whilst this particular measure was abolished in 1975, it saw the first attempt to focus housing finance away from government subsidies and towards rents, thus limiting government's subsidy liability.

The second change was the replacement of all existing government subsidy liability with a new deficit subsidy which was calculated annually on the basis of a local authority's income and expenditure. This meant that government was no longer committed to subsidies into the future and, moreover, it now had leverage over rents in that it could make certain assumptions on rent levels when setting the annual subsidy. Central government now had a mechanism with which to control activity.

The third change was no less important, seeing the introduction of a mandatory rent rebate scheme for council tenants and tenants in non-furnished private rented accommodation. The significance of this change was that ability to pay was no longer a bar on access to council housing. Over time, this change, when taken together with policies such as the right to buy and the homelessness provisions introduced in 1977, has had the effect of changing the demographic make-up of council tenants, away from a dominance of the affluent working classes and towards those who are economically inactive.

The importance of the 1972 Act, then, was, first, that it gave government a mechanism with which to control activity, but, second, it saw the start of the move away from object subsidies to subject subsidies. As we shall see in the discussion on specific tenures, both central control and the use of personal subsidies have proved to be long-term trends.

A further significant development in the 1970s was the introduction for the 1977/8 financial year of the requirement for local authorities to submit housing investment programmes (HIPs) detailing their assessment of housing need and a costed programme of works for housing capital expenditure including items such as improvement grants. This was presented as a means for rational planning, whereby scarce resources could be matched up to the most pressing local needs. But the HIP system developed during the 1980s and 1990s into a further means of central control. Government achieved this by establishing, through the HIP system, the priorities under which local authorities must bid for funds – although this use of a planning tool to control activity might not be so surprising when one remembers that the HIP system was introduced during a period of public expenditure cuts. Planning becomes much more of an issue when resources are tight.

The 1970s also saw the end of the consensus that had largely existed in housing policy since the late 1940s. This became clear in 1979 after the election of a Conservative government. The Conservatives began to shift away from a public-sector solution, instead seeing council housing as the problem. They shifted policy more towards the promotion of owner occupation. Whilst it is the case that most post-war governments including Attlee's, elected in 1945, promoted owner occupation as a desirable tenure, all these governments did so alongside a policy of mass public housebuilding. Most governments saw owner occupation as an important aspiration for middle-class and, from the 1960s onwards, working-class households. Yet this did not detract from their support of publicly rented housing.

However, the Thatcher government elected in 1979 took a somewhat different view, seeing the two tenures as competing rather than complementing each other. As a result, after 1979 local authorities lost their position at the centre of housing policy and saw their stock decline, owing to a shift in subsidies. But also by the end of the 1970s, politicians could claim that the crude shortfall in dwellings had been met and therefore the key housing problem was no longer that of shortage, but of quality.

This shift in the balance away from local authorities had been signalled several years earlier when the Housing Act 1974 gave the Housing Corporation the powers to make grants to associations that covered most of the costs of development. From 1974, housing associations began to grow in significance as social landlords, to the extent that the Thatcher government could place them at the centre of policy from 1988 onwards.

Conservative housing policy in the 1980s and 1990s

The main plank of Conservative housing policy in the 1980s and 1990s was to promote owner occupation as a tenure offering choice, and independence from state interference. The government also increasingly saw local authorities as the cause of housing problems, rather than the solution to them. Therefore one can characterise government policy as pursuing an increase in owner occupation at the expense of local authority housing. Of course, the primary example of this policy is the right to buy (RTB), which allows existing council (and some housing association) tenants to purchase their own home at a discount. But the Conservatives also made some major changes to the management of local authority housing finance through the Housing Act 1980.

This Act reformed revenue funding, with the aim of further increasing the level of control exercised by central government. It did this by introducing notional HRAs in which the Department of the Environment[1] (DoE)

---

1 The Department of the Environment was renamed the Department of the Environment, Transport and the Regions in 1997.

determined what was legitimate expenditure for each local authority and thus what income it needed to fund this spending. The difference between income and expenditure was to be made up by subsidy. The importance of this notional HRA was that the DoE assumed that each local authority stuck to these income and expenditure figures, and set housing subsidy accordingly. These notional accounts were not what each local authority did spend or wished to spend, but rather were what the government felt an authority ought to be spending if it was doing an efficient and effective job. A local authority was at liberty to increase its income and expenditure above the notional level, but it would not receive any extra subsidy. The effect of this mechanism was to allow government to influence rents by manipulating notional income and expenditure and the level of subsidy. This influence was intended, of course, to force rents up.

However, as income was typically deemed to rise faster than expenditure, by 1987/8 only 95 of 374 local authorities were receiving subsidy. The problem with this mechanism was that it was effective only so long as subsidy was being paid. Once local authorities went out of subsidy, government lost any leverage it had previously had over rents. There were other problems with the funding mechanism for local authorities in the 1980s that the Conservatives felt needed attention.

First, the 1980 system allowed local authorities to transfer funds to and from their rate fund. This allowed them either to subsidise their rents or to keep the rates artificially low. In either case the government felt this allowed authorities to hide inefficiencies in their management. For instance, it was argued that some local authorities had little incentive to chase arrears and minimise voids if they could draw on the rates to fund the HRA. Furthermore, as the block grant system subsidising the rate fund operated on a different basis than housing subsidy it was possible for twenty-four local authorities in 1987/8 to make contributions to the rate fund out of the HRA and to receive housing subsidy because their notional HRA was in deficit.

A further issue was that government was concerned with the growth in rent rebates and the consequent effect on the Department of Social Security (DSS) budget. This was due to several factors. The 1980s had seen a massive increase in unemployment. Also, the government was concerned with demographic trends such as the growth in elderly-person households. The 1980s therefore saw the residualisation of council housing, which meant that an increasing proportion of tenants were economically inactive and thus in receipt of benefit. The government therefore was eager to find some means whereby the cost of rent rebates could be minimised.

On the capital side the government felt it needed to deal with the growth of local authority capital receipts, which had arisen largely from RTB sales. As early as 1983, government had attempted to control capital receipts by limiting their use to a specific proportion per annum (20 per cent from 1985 onwards), but it had consistently failed to predict accurately the level of spending because authorities were able to spend 20 per cent of receipts accumulating in the year plus 20 per cent of accumulated receipts from previous years. The government wanted to control this so-called *cascade effect*. There was a further problem with capital receipts in that they did not necessarily accrue in areas of greatest housing need. Indeed, there was negative correlation between the level of housing need and RTB sales. The government sought a mechanism to deal with this. Finally, government felt the need to close certain loopholes which had been exploited in the existing legislation. In particular, the government could control only borrowing by local authorities, and not other credit or leaseback arrangements. Some local authorities, e.g. Liverpool, undertook complicated leaseback arrangements whereby the cost of development was met by a bank or financial institution, with the local authority then making annual repayments similar to those under a hire purchase agreement.

As a result of these problems on both the revenue and capital sides, the Local Government and Housing Act 1989 was introduced. This still forms the basis of revenue and capital funding.

The government also felt there were problems with the manner in which housing associations were supported. The system introduced in 1974 was effective in producing dwellings of a high quality at reasonable rents. The form of subsidy can be seen as a deficit or residual one. It aimed to enable housing associations to cover the costs of a particular scheme from the first year's income from that scheme. However, this meant that it was possible to determine the exact level of grant only on the completion of the scheme. Grant was determined on the basis of the annual rent less allowances for voids and management and maintenance. Any residual income would form an annual repayment to the Housing Corporation. This annual payment was capitalised into a loan. The rest of the capital cost was covered by grant.

On average, housing association grant (HAG) was between 75 and 85 per cent but could conceivably be 100 per cent if rent only equalled or was less than allowable expenditure on management and maintenance (see Chapter 5 for a fuller discussion).

This system proved effective in terms of developing new dwellings and rehabilitating existing stock. Indeed, from the housing associations' point of view, the system might have been bureaucratic and unwieldy, but it was relatively risk free. However, from the government's perspective, it had a number of problems. First, housing associations had no incentive to economise, especially as the grant level was set at the end of the development process. In addition, associations could claim revenue deficit subsidies if expenditure on a scheme was greater than rent income. Second, the system was felt to be too bureaucratic and in need of streamlining. Third, it was felt that housing associations were enjoying a very high level of subsidy. Through a combination of capital and revenue subsidies it was possible to claim subsidy in excess of 100 per cent. Lastly, there was no relationship between rents and the costs of a scheme, as rents were set by the independent rent officer service. Housing association tenancies prior to 1989 were secure tenancies offering a controlled rent that could be amended only every second year by an amount determined by the rent officer. Rents were set according to local rent levels rather than the costs incurred in developing the scheme. The government introduced the Housing Act 1988 in an attempt to deal with these problems.

The 1988 and 1989 Acts still provide the basis for the current system of housing finance, even though some changes have been made, most recently those relating to local authority capital and resource accounting. Therefore it seems appropriate to end this historical summary here. However, there is a further point that perhaps needs making. The 1980s and 1990s appear to indicate a changing role for social housing, and this is recognised in its financing. There is a belief, held by government at least, that there is no great need for new social housing in many parts of the country, in that the historical shortages have been made up. In consequence, the emphasis is on the management and maintenance of social housing. In other words, the priorities are now on quality and access instead of quantity.

What has become increasingly important is *how* housing is funded to maintain and improve the quality, especially as government funding is limited, and *who* should be doing this managing. Since 1988 one of the aims of housing finance can be seen as encouraging the break-up of council housing as a tenure, with housing associations and the private sector playing an increasing role in management and what new building is seen as necessary. This has involved large-scale and trickle transfers of local authority stock and attempts to develop forms of funding which do not require government borrowing.

Finally, we should not overstate the role of government in this historical development of subsidies. Government does not operate in a vacuum, but rather it reacts to phenomena and events which impose themselves on it. Thus much of the government action we have discussed above has come about because of changing conditions and circumstances, which it has tried to control or moderate, but which government certainly neither initiated nor necessarily fully understood. Of at least equal significance has been the impact of external effects, from extreme situations like war through to long-term demographic trends and heightened affluence.

I am not suggesting that government can have no impact, nor that we necessarily need less government action. My concern here is rather to suggest that government is only one of the players. It might be more or less significant at certain times, but this doesn't mean it can control events. Indeed, somewhat paradoxically perhaps, might not the continued attempts to control housing processes indicate the relative impotence government has when it comes up against external forces?

ACTIVITY 3.2

Give three examples of how changes to housing subsidies have had a major effect on the type of housing provided.

Summary

In this chapter I have:

- looked at the reasons why there was only limited government intervention in the nineteenth century;

- examined how intervention developed out of the First World War;

- considered the impact and nature of government intervention, particularly rent controls in the private rented sector and the borrowing and subsidy regime for local authorities;

- discussed the development of mass council building after 1945;

- examined the reasons for the ending of the post-1945 consensus over housing policy in the 1980s and 1990s;

- considered the change from object to subject subsidies and how this has altered the function of social housing; and

- discussed the importance of unexpected consequences in the development of complex housing finance systems.

Further reading

There are many works on the history of housing policy. Gauldie (1974) covers the social issues well, but only goes up to 1914. Burnett (1986) gives a longer coverage, but is more concerned with levels of amenity. Daunton (1987) offers a brief but cogent political history of housing up to 1987. The most detailed historical survey of government housing policy is provided by Holmans (1987), but this does not go beyond the end of the 1970s. Malpass and Murie (1999) offer a brisk survey of housing policy in their early chapters and Malpass (1990) provides a good detailed historical survey of local authority revenue finance.

4 Local authorities

- Central–local government relations and the increasing centralisation of political control of housing
- The local authority capital finance system and how this relates to issues such as stock transfer and private finance
- The revenue finance regime, including housing revenue account (HRA) subsidy, rents and the introduction of resource accounting
- The future prospects and problems facing local authorities

Introduction

Council housing has historically been the mainstay of social housing in Britain. Over 6 million dwellings were built by local authorities during the twentieth century (compared to just under a million by housing associations), and by the mid-1970s a third of households lived in council accommodation. Yet since then council housing has been in decline, in terms of the size of the stock, the amount of government subsidy spent on it and, as a consequence of the last two points, in terms of quality.

It would be easy to suggest that this situation has come about by a process of neglect, either on the part of government or on the part of local authorities themselves. Indeed, the former Conservative governments, particularly in the 1980s, liked to portray local authorities as inefficient and ineffective bureaucracies incapable of managing their own affairs (DoE, 1987). On the other hand, bodies such as the Chartered Institute of Housing and the Local Government Association have been quick to criticise central government for causing a backlog in repairs through its continued cuts in housing capital spending and the restrictions it has placed on the use of accumulated capital receipts.

But, whilst both sides to this argument might have something of a case, I do not think that the decline in council housing has come about because it has been neglected. Indeed, the opposite is the case. When looking at the actions of central government, the past twenty years have seen not a reduction in involvement, but instead an increase in centralisation and control.

Government has not neglected local authority housing, but has rather sought to *nationalise* it so that it can be used to meet its aims. The problem, however, has been that the improvement and further development of council housing have not featured in those aims. As we saw in Chapter 3, since the mid-1970s both Conservative and Labour governments have sought to reduce public expenditure and shift the burden of provision onto the private sector. Thus, in terms of housing policy, we have seen the increased importance of housing associations (using private finance) and owner occupation.

What this shows is that it is not merely whether government is involved or not that is important, but in what manner government intervenes. Government now intervenes in council housing in order to try to control it, rather than to encourage it. Some might argue that it would be better for government to have pursued a policy of benign neglect rather than the policy it in fact has pursued over the past twenty years. At least then local authorities could have pursued policies suitable for their own local needs free from outside interference. Instead, government intervention can be said to have actually been detrimental to the interests of local authorities and their tenants, because national concerns have consistently trumped local issues.

The Blair government, elected in 1997, has now set out its agenda for local authorities. This agenda involves a move to a more business-orientated approach with the introduction of resource accounting. But at the same time there is to be no let-up with regard to central scrutiny, with rent policy being directed from Westminster and the use of bodies such as the Housing Inspectorate to ensure that standards are met. Therefore, whilst new policies are to be introduced, it appears that the relationship between central and local government will still be an unequal one.

In this chapter I shall discuss the current and future financial arrangements which govern local authority housing, but I wish to do so in the context of this somewhat negative form of intervention. Therefore I shall begin by looking at the relationship between central and local government.

This is a rather long chapter, primarily because I have chosen to look at the role of central government here rather than in a separate chapter or in one of the introductory ones. The main theme of this book is that central government has tightened its grip on housing and has effectively nationalised what were local resources. This issue is best dealt with in context. Centralisation in housing has been most marked in the local authority sector, which was and is the largest rented sector and the one using the most resources. I believe therefore that the length of this chapter is justified, in that the discussion about the role of government with regard to local authorities sets the context for the discussion of the other housing sectors later in the book.

ACTIVITY 4.1

Make a list, in order of importance, of the activities of a local authority housing department. Where does the money come from?

Central government control

Despite the fact that Britain does not have a formal written constitution, we can see that it is a *unitary* rather than a federal state. This means that political power has only one source, and that is, formally, 'the Crown in Parliament'. It is Parliament in which political power is vested. Only Parliament may enact legislation and it alone has tax-raising powers. Thus, for local authorities to do anything, they must have obtained the express permission of Parliament. Indeed, local authorities exist only because of the specific acts of Parliament which created them.

In practice, power is exercised by the majority party, which forms the government, with the party leader as the Prime Minister. Whilst Parliament exists to represent the electorate and to hold the government to account, the government, through party links, largely controls Parliament.

The British constitution, because it is unwritten, is determined by precedent and the legitimacy expressed through general elections. A government is elected on the basis of a manifesto, which it then seeks to implement. This means that the government of the day has considerable power to determine and change policy. The constitutional position may be changed simply by a majority vote in both houses of Parliament, as occurred in 1998 with the creation of a Scottish Parliament and Welsh Assembly, and in 2000 with the removal of most of the hereditary peers from the House of Lords. A further change that may have a considerable effect in the future is the incorporation of the European Convention on Human Rights into Scottish law in 1999 and English law in 2000. This means that for the first time British citizens have defined rights that the state has a duty to respect and protect. However, there is nothing constitutionally to stop a future Parliament from taking these rights away.

The only real internal restraints on the actions of a government are tradition, popularity and competence. There are traditions, in terms of how Parliament operates and the roles of institutions and officers of the state, which are accepted and respected. These traditions may appear absurd. For instance, there is a tradition that an MP puts on a top hat when he or she wishes to make a point of order. Also, the House of Commons normally doesn't start its working day until mid-afternoon and then frequently works through into the night. Other traditions are more serious, such as the convention that the unelected House of Lords does not block a manifesto commitment of the government.

There are, however, two factors that might limit a government's freedom of action. First, whilst an elected government, which commands a majority in both houses of Parliament, can do much of what it wishes, any government must be aware of what is popular or unpopular with voters. Of course, this is particularly the case when an election approaches (and this is the reason why governments tend to take the difficult decisions at the start of a parliamentary term rather than the end). Thus, even though the Conservatives elected in 1987 had a majority in the House of Commons of over a hundred, they were forced to replace the hugely unpopular community charge (poll tax) in 1991 with something more acceptable. This was seen as necessary even though the community charge had been part of the manifesto it had been elected on in 1987. (This was probably the only time when local government finance has caused riots on the streets!)

Second, any government's policies might fall prey to external effects beyond its control. For instance, a downturn in the world economy will affect Britain despite the best efforts of government. Indeed, as the British economy becomes more interlocked into the global economy, this will become more of an issue. The future of the British car industry is now decided in boardrooms in Chicago, Tokyo or Seoul rather than Oxford or Coventry.

The issue of competence refers to two distinct things. First, one can talk of competence in the sense of how far government does what it says it is going to and runs the country properly. In this sense, the Major government between 1992 and 1997 was frequently seen as incompetent in that it appeared to lurch from one crisis to another. For instance, it was able to get the Maastrich Treaty through Parliament only by threatening its own side with a general election at a time when the Conservatives were trailing in the opinion polls.

Central–local relations

But competence can also be used to discuss the proper role of government. Certain necessary activities should quite obviously be undertaken by central government. National defence is one such example. However, there are other necessary activities that are better run by other bodies. This might be because they relate to individual choices and thus are best left to private companies, or because they depend upon an understanding of local needs and issues. One such issue is housing, which historically has been provided locally because local needs and priorities differ. Thus housing provision has been seen as one activity that should be delegated to the lowest level of competence. Housing has, then, been built, managed and (to an extent) paid for locally through local authorities.

Indeed, there are many activities that are seen as necessary, but are provided and managed by so-called *intermediate institutions*. These are bodies that operate at a level between the state and individual citizens. They may be formal bodies such as local authorities, but they also include non-governmental organisations such as trade unions and churches. As was suggested in Chapter 1, it is important to realise that whilst central government makes policy and is the key regulator, it often relies on intermediate institutions such as local authorities and the Housing Corporation to actually implement and manage policies.

However, the relationship between central government and intermediate institutions has changed since the 1970s. One of the central tenets of Thatcherite Conservative ideology, which dominated government in the 1980s, was the need to limit and control the role of intermediate institutions. This was because they were seen as forming a barrier between the state and its subjects (Devigne, 1994). Instead of seeing institutions such as local authorities as playing a positive role in the development of policy, the Conservative governments saw them as one of the causes of Britain's post-war economic and political decline. The Conservatives believed that Britain was becoming ungovernable because of the diverse demands being placed upon the state by groups, such as the trade unions, and institutions. There was perceived to be a breakdown in central authority. Thus a key role for government was to reassert the authority of the state in the face of these competing demands. One can see the effect of this in the public and social policies of the Thatcher governments, which attacked the roles of bodies such as the trade unions, professions such as teachers, and, of course, local authorities as an alternative source of power.

Another facet of Thatcherism, however, was the pursuance of individual economic freedom. Individuals were encouraged to take more decisions for themselves without reliance on the state (King, 1996). However, it was argued that this economic freedom could be achieved only by a strong central government. Gamble (1988) has shown how the Conservatives under Margaret Thatcher could not trust anyone but themselves to undertake their aims of reducing the role of the state in the lives of individuals. Intermediate institutions, such as local authorities, could not be trusted to carry out the process of liberalisation themselves, because of the vested interests they represented. There was thus the paradox of government taking more powers on itself in order to liberate individuals from the effects of (local) government.

This paradox has been particularly evident with regard to local authorities and their control over local housing. Jenkins (1995) has suggested that the centralisation of the control over council housing by the Thatcher and Major governments has been one of the largest nationalisations carried out by any government. His point is that despite a rhetoric of individualism and choice, central government has taken over the control of what were hitherto local assets owned by locally elected and locally accountable political bodies.

Indeed, despite the unitary nature of the British state, there has been a strong tradition of localism in Britain. Local authorities (in their previous incarnations as parishes and city corporations) have a long tradition, dating back to the seventeenth century, of providing local services for local people that were paid for locally. These services include poor relief, sanitation, education and, of course, housing. The housing stock was seen as a local resource for the benefit of the local community. Whilst it had been provided with the help of central government subsidies, there had also been a considerable amount of local input through the rates and rents. It was quite clearly understood that the housing stock belonged to the local authority, which was accountable to the local electorate for its management and maintenance.

ACTIVITY 4.2

What are the advantages of central control of housing?

The end of localism

But the idea of localism was not respected by the Conservatives and did not survive for long into the 1980s. They justified their distrust of local initiative on several grounds:

- First, they believed that local authorities were extravagant overspenders that could potentially jeopardise central government's public spending plans. They were able to maintain this perception of extravagance even though local authority spending had been in decline since 1976 and was largely under control, unlike, as Jenkins (1995) points out, central government spending, both before and after 1979.
- Second, as their policies began to have some effect, the Conservatives had to deal with the potential and actual political opposition from local authorities, particularly those controlled by the Labour and Liberal (later Liberal Democrat) parties. Of course, as spending by local authorities was cut and measures such as rate-capping were introduced, the size of the political opposition grew and thus the need to control the activities of local authorities became more acute. It would not be unfair to suggest that the Conservatives' perception of local authorities became self-justifying, in that their distrust of local government merely created an environment of mutual suspicion and opposition.
- Third, Conservative ideology was concerned with helping households exercise choice and responsibility for their actions rather than relying on the state. This manifested itself in terms of the support of owner occupation and the dislike of the supposed bureaucratic forms of allocation and management used by local government (DoE, 1987). Local authorities were not seen as being sufficiently responsive to tenants' wishes and offering choice. In many ways this was a caricature of the relationship between local authorities and their tenants. Whilst 1.5 million tenants have exercised their right to buy, this may be as much an indication of the government's generosity, in terms of the discounts offered, as a comment on the management of council housing. What might have been more demonstrative of tenants' views was the abject failure of the government's Tenants' Choice proposals introduced in 1989 giving council tenants the opportunity to choose an alternative landlord. Only one transfer was made under this scheme, and that involved the Conservative London Borough of Westminster, which wished to sell off an estate in the face of tenant opposition.

This attitude towards council housing was manifested in the attempt to break up local authorities' housing stock to give people the choice and opportunity of owner occupation. In time the policy developed through the use of the private sector through housing associations and private finance, and initiatives such as Housing Action Trusts, Tenants' Choice and Compulsory Competitive Tendering. However, these policies could be achieved only through the centralisation of power and control in Whitehall and Westminster.

None of these policies developed because of a groundswell of opinion from tenants, or indeed because local authorities themselves considered them to be needed. They derived from the central government's somewhat jaundiced perception of the role of local authorities.

No change since 1997

In some ways the attitude of the Labour government elected in 1997 appears similar. Despite the fact that the Labour Party has traditionally been more favourable towards local authorities, Labour made a manifesto commitment to maintain the Major government's spending plans and priorities for its first two years in office. In fact the government managed to underspend in those two years. In addition, the Labour government has largely retained the capping of local authority expenditure and income, despite arguing against the measure whilst in opposition. The outcomes of the first comprehensive spending review announced in July 1998, which signalled the full, but phased, release of accumulated capital receipts and the announcement of the New Deal for Communities, appeared to offer resources to specifically locally led initiatives. The second comprehensive spending review in July 2000 saw an increase in the resources made available to local authorities, but the restriction in the first two years of the Parliament meant that spending overall is no greater than the long-term average under the Conservatives in the 1980s and 1990s.

Nor has there been any move away from central direction since 1997. Local authorities may have been given more resources since 1997, but it is still central government that determines the priorities and sets the performance standards by which local authorities are to be judged. Indeed, a whole new regulatory framework based around Best Value and the Housing Inspectorate has been developed to ensure that this is the case. I would suggest, then, that there has been no lessening of central regulation and control since 1997.

One of the principal effects of centralisation has been to stop local authorities from building new dwellings. This is not because they are legally forbidden to do so. It is rather because their spending allocations are determined on the basis of whether they meet the priorities and expectations of central government. A local authority may choose to ignore government priorities, but it is likely to be financially punished by government in the future. As the former housing minister Hilary Armstrong said in 1998, with regard to local choice:

> It's very much about a local choice – but local choices have consequences. The consequences may mean it is much harder for me to argue with the chancellor that the money is being well-spent and he should keep the flow going.
>
> (quoted in Blake, 1998, p. 20)

The implication is that local authorities can do what they like, but they will receive funding only if this concurs with what central government wishes them to do.

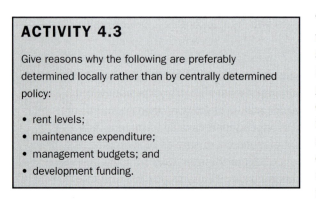

ACTIVITY 4.3

Give reasons why the following are preferably determined locally rather than by centrally determined policy:

- rent levels;
- maintenance expenditure;
- management budgets; and
- development funding.

This raises a key issue in understanding local authority housing finance. Since the early 1980s central government has sought to control councils and achieve its ends not through legal sanctions (even though these exist, and councillors can be surcharged and disbarred from office), but through financial leverage. It is central government's control over finance that constrains local authorities. We now need to look at how central government attempts to maintain control and use its financial leverage.

Capital and revenue finance

Before looking at specific finance mechanisms, we need to make the distinction between capital and revenue finance. Revenue is that finance needed to manage the day-to-day running costs of the housing service. It therefore covers staff salaries, management and maintenance costs, and other administrative costs. Revenue income largely comes from two sources: rent income and government subsidy.

Capital finance is that which enhances the asset value of the housing stock. It therefore deals with the acquisition and development of land, buildings, plant and machinery. It also covers those repairs funded through borrowing and capital grants and advances. Hence it comprises items intended to last several years, whereas revenue finance is for immediate or short-term items.

However, there is some overlap between capital and revenue. For instance, the historic purpose of housing subsidies was to assist with repaying borrowing and interest payments, even though these subsidies are credited to the housing revenue account (HRA). Also, many local authorities before 1989 used their capital receipts to fund routine maintenance. This is no longer possible, but it is still possible for an authority to make a contribution to capital from its HRA.

One of the undoubted effects of the system of resource accounting introduced in 2001 will be the blurring of the distinction between capital and revenue by focusing revenue expenditure on maintaining and improving the housing stock. This, as we shall see on p. 64, will involve the transfer of what was once capital expenditure (basic credit approvals) into revenue expenditure (major repairs allowance).

This blurring of the distinction between revenue and capital implies a changed role for local authorities. No longer are local authorities mass housebuilders. They are rather perceived now as housing managers whose main responsibility is to preserve and improve what the 2000 green paper (DETR, 2000a) calls a national asset. As we shall see, resource accounting aims to institutionalise this perception.

Housing investment programmes (HIPs)

The starting point to understanding the capital finance system is the HIP system. As we saw in Chapter 3, controls were introduced in the financial year 1977/8 requiring each local authority to submit an annual housing strategy and a housing investment programme statement. The purpose of the housing strategy statement is to outline local needs and the HIP statement is a costed capital works programme aimed at meeting these needs. HIPs allowed central government to set a limit to total local authority housing investment across the country and then to distribute it to individual local authorities on the basis of their relative needs. Thus it was recognised that financial resources were limited and needed to be targeted to where needs were greatest.

Thus the HIP system began as a planning mechanism. But it was quickly turned into a means of control. Government was able not only to set the total level of financial resources available, but to set priorities for spending at the local level. Thus in the 1980s and 1990s the HIP system was used as a means of controlling activity and setting priorities according to the needs of central government, rather than being a rational planning tool, or indeed a means of allowing local authorities to inform the centre of their priorities.

HIPs used to be allocated solely via a Generalised Needs Index (GNI), which aims to show relative needs based on a variety of social, economic and demographic measures. From the early 1990s the Conservative government introduced criteria based on performance and efficiency into the allocative mechanism. For the financial year 1997/8 it went so far as to allocate the HIP settlement on a competitive basis according to the DoE's determination of housing need and whether a local authority met certain performance and efficiency criteria. However, upon taking office, the Blair government made a partial return to allocations on the basis of need through GNIs, but with 50 per cent still to be allocated on the basis of performance. Thus each HIP bid is assessed against guidelines aimed to compare local authority performance and ensure good practice. HIP bids are usually submitted in late summer, with the funding decisions announced around Christmas. A local authority's financial year begins in April.

Local authorities do have some discretion in terms of assessing local needs. However, they do this within the context of clear national priorities outlined by government. This is how central government is able to prevent local authorities from building and to ensure that they concentrate on maintaining their own stock and on pursuing a strategic enabling role.

It should be noted that HIP allocations are *permissions to spend and borrow*, and not grants. Local authorities do not usually receive grants but must borrow or use their accumulated capital receipts. Those grants they do receive may be used only for private-sector initiatives such as improvement grants. Revenue subsidy, of course, has the purpose of offsetting debt repayments. In this way local authorities are treated differently from housing associations, which receive direct grants to cover a proportion of their development costs.

However, even though HIP allocations are permissions to incur debt, they are still deemed to be public expenditure and thus a matter for central government control. Local authorities are part of government, providing vital public services such as education, social services and housing. No one, least of all the financial markets, believes that central government will allow a local authority to fail financially. Thus the Treasury effectively backs local authority borrowing pound for pound and thus assumes it as spent. This, of course, gives local authorities a degree of financial security, but it also means they have to accept central government control. As we shall see on p. 60, there has been a lot of debate about whether local authorities should be released from public spending restrictions and be allowed to borrow from the private sector without Treasury backing. The 2000 housing green paper (DETR, 2000a) and the 2000 local authority finance green paper (DETR, 2000b) both appear to be offering a limited opportunity for this.

The post-1989 capital system

The current framework for the capital funding and control system was determined by the Local Government and Housing Act 1989. The government announced its intention to reform capital finance in 2001 by the introduction of a single pot for capital finance. In addition, the green paper on local authority finance published in late 2000 (DETR, 2000b) offers tentative proposals for further reform. As was mentioned on p. 53, resource accounting will also affect capital finance. All these proposals will be discussed later in the chapter. However, the 1989 system will still substantially be in operation until 2002 at least. Even then, the government's means of controlling capital will still be those established in the 1989 Act.

In response to individual local authorities' HIP bids, the Department of the Environment, Transport and the Regions (as the Department of the Environment became in 1997) allocates an *Annual Capital Guideline* (ACG). This is the notional amount that the government believes the local authority needs to spend on capital works. The aim of the ACG system is to achieve a 'fair' distribution of resources, whereby credit approvals are offset by accumulated capital receipts. Thus, in principle, those local authorities with large receipts will receive fewer basic credit approvals, and vice versa.

The funding to meet the ACG may come from three sources: borrowing and credit; government grants; and capital receipts.

Borrowing and credit

Each local authority is given a credit limit in the form of *basic credit approvals* (BCAs) for the year. This includes both borrowing and any other credit arrangements such as leaseback arrangements. A local authority may also be allocated *supplementary credit approvals* (SCAs) for special projects and one-off items of expenditure. SCAs are usually allocated on the basis of specific bids for projects. For example, SCAs might be allocated to fund cash incentive schemes offering tenants a cash sum to buy a property in the private sector. It is not unusual for a local authority's SCAs to exceed its BCAs, especially since the introduction of the Capital receipts initiative (see below).

Government grants

The government gives each local authority *specified capital grants* (SCGs), which relate to the authority's work in and with the private sector, particularly improvement grants.

Capital receipts

Until 1997 the use of capital receipts was limited to 25 per cent of right-to-buy sales and 50 per cent of land sales. The DETR estimates the amount of receipts likely to be used by a local authority in the year. These are referred to as *receipts taken into account* (RTIAs). In July 1997 the government announced that local authorities could spend additional receipts, and the comprehensive spending review in 1998 determined allocations until 2001/2, which will see the full release of accumulated receipts. This money has been allocated by additional SCAs on the basis of one-third according to accumulated receipts set aside and two-thirds general housing need. The effect of the Capital receipts initiative was to return capital spending to its 1996/7 level. It thus merely restores the cuts imposed in the final year of the Major government. Thus whilst spending has increased since 1996, it has only been returned to the trend of the 1990s.

In terms of determining how resources are allocated, the crucial factor is the level of usable capital receipts. This is achieved by the application of the following formula:

ACG – RTIA – SCG = BCAs

where:

ACG = annual capital guideline;

RTIA = receipts taken into account;

SCG = specified capital grants; and

BCAs = basic credit approvals.

Therefore the government is able to offset the allocation of BCAs by the level of capital receipts (RTIA), allowing for a more rational national allocation of scarce resources. Thus those authorities with relatively high levels of accumulated receipts will receive fewer BCAs than those that have smaller receipts. Of course, once the accumulated receipts have been spent, this formula will not operate so effectively. However, the shift to resource accounting, with much of the ACG being converted into a major repairs allowance, will mean that the old formula for funding will no longer apply in any case. This assumes, as seems likely, that local authorities will need to continue spending on major repairs in the long term.

ACTIVITY 4.4

Using the formula ACG – SCG – RTIA = BCA, calculate the amount of BCAs where:

ACG = £5 million
SCG = £0.5 million
RTIA = £1.75 million

Controlling capital

The 1989 system means that central government has the ability to control local authorities in a number of ways:

- by restricting and directing the spending of capital receipts according to a national formula;
- by taking estimated capital receipts into account when deciding on the ACG;
- by controlling borrowing and credit arrangements through BCAs;
- through the total size of the allocation for capital spending; and
- by establishing priorities as part of the HIP process.

This is all in addition to the Best Value regime backed up by the Housing Inspectorate. Indeed, the 2000 green paper on local government finance

(DETR, 2000b) specifically mentions the possibility of withdrawing funding from poorly performing authorities.

What the 1989 system didn't do was allow local authorities to manage their stock of dwellings according to their own local priorities. There have been many who have argued that the 1989 system should be reformed to give greater autonomy to local authorities. We therefore need to look at some of these reform proposals, especially those put forward by the Blair government.

Reforming capital finance

As with many aspects of housing, capital finance is facing changes on several fronts. After accepting the Conservative government's spending plans for the first two years of its term of office, the Blair government published new proposals on capital finance (other than the Capital receipts initiative) only in late 1998, and these proposals came into force only in 2001 or later. However, some proposed reforms, such as stock transfer, are developments of long-standing policies begun by the Conservatives.

What this shows is that there was a considerable degree of continuity in housing policy in the 1990s. This is partly because of the complexity of housing systems and the political impossibility of a 'big bang' approach to reform. But it also indicates a considerable degree of consensus about the role of local authorities and other social landlords. Hence we should not necessarily see the 1997 election as offering a dramatic change in policy. Rather, as we shall see in Chapter 9, there is more consistency between Conservative and Labour policy than either party would readily wish to admit. In particular, two of the issues to be discussed below – stock transfer and the Private Finance Initiative – are indicative of this continuity, having begun under the Conservatives and been developed further by the Labour government.

Stock transfer

The first stock transfers – now referred to as large-scale voluntary transfers (LSVT) – were a spontaneous attempt to circumvent the 1989 restrictions, which involved the creation of a new housing association to which the local authority's stock was transferred. Whilst this allowed for new development through a mix of private and public finance, it could be achieved only by a virtual act of suicide, in that the housing department effectively ceased to exist apart from a small number of staff dealing with the strategic enabling function.

The Major government after the 1992 election was quick to control LSVT. This was done for three reasons:

- the possible effect of the release of capital receipts from the transfer, giving some authorities a large increase in their usable receipts over and above the annual capital guideline;
- the housing benefit implications, because housing association tenants on housing benefit are fully funded by government subsidy, whilst councils do not necessarily receive the full cost of rent rebates for their tenants (see p. 68); and
- the possible squeeze on the mixed-funded programme of housing associations, which might have been unable to compete with LSVT associations for the available private finance.

LSVT was controlled initially by the imposition of a 20 per cent levy and a quota limiting the stock transferred in any one year. However, the policy was broadly amenable with the government's intentions, and once it was regulated, it was encouraged. By 1997 the Conservatives had included transfer proposals as a criterion for HIP funding. Whilst this approach on transfers was not followed by the Labour government, transfers have continued, and the 2000 green paper (DETR, 2000a) announced a substantial increase in transfers to 200,000 per annum. This means that the size of the local authority sector is likely to decrease considerably in the first decade of the twenty-first century.

Whilst most LSVT authorities have been relatively small rural local authorities, recently several large urban local authorities such as Coventry, Tameside and Birmingham have progressed transfer proposals involving some or all of their stock. Between 1998 and 2000, 406,587 dwellings from eighty-four English local authorities were transferred to new LSVT landlords (Wilcox, 2000).

The use of private finance

There has been much debate since the mid-1990s about whether local authorities should be able to borrow without its being deemed public expenditure. This is the situation enjoyed by housing associations, and many have argued that local authorities, which generally have a more secure asset base than most housing associations, should be able to act in a similar manner. The view of central government, though, has been that the financial markets would assume that the Treasury would bale out a troubled local authority, which, after all, has powers only because of an act of Parliament.

One proposal canvassed by bodies such as the Chartered Institute of Housing involved changing the government's definition of public spending to allow local authorities to borrow without its counting as public spending. The proposal involves a switch from the Public Sector Borrowing Requirement (PSBR),[1] which is calculated to include all borrowing, including that by local authorities and public-sector trading bodies, to the method used in Germany and other European countries of the *General Government Financial Deficit* (GGFD), which counts only central government borrowing and not that of local government or public-sector bodies. If this were adopted, local authorities could borrow in the same way as housing associations. But despite this receiving a lot of attention, both the Conservative and Labour governments have ruled out such a change.

An alternative proposal, and one taken more seriously by government, has been to set up arm's-length companies that would manage council housing. Being separate from the local authority, they could then raise finance in the private sector. An example of this followed the Housing Act 1996, which allowed for local housing companies to be established to take over, manage and improve council stock. The companies would have only a minority of local authority representatives on their board and thus the housing would no longer be under the direct control of the local authority. Local housing companies would use private-sector finance to carry out improvements to the stock, but could also gain access to public support through the *Estates Renewal Challenge Fund* (ERCF), set up to disburse £314 million over three years (1996/7–1998/9). The potential significance of local housing companies for government was that the private finance raised does not count as public spending. From the point of view of local authorities, they could use the asset value of the stock as security for the raising of as much as £60 billion in private finance. However, the first attempt to transfer property to a local housing company in Sandwell was voted down by tenants (*Housing Today*, 25 September 1997).

---

1 Subsequently the PSBR has been renamed the Public Sector Net Cash Requirement (PSNCR).

Following the 1998 comprehensive spending review, the ERCF was abolished, with resources channelled through the Single Regeneration Budget and the New Deal for Communities. Therefore local housing companies never really developed as a concept.

However, the attempt to introduce private finance into local authority has taken on a new emphasis following the 2000 housing green paper (DETR, 2000a). The government objective is to separate a local authority's strategic and management roles. Therefore, not only is the government encouraging stock transfers and the Private Finance Initiative, it also wishes to see the establishment of arm's-length companies to manage council housing. The green paper offers the promise that the best-performing local authorities would be given extra scope to borrow. It also appears that the government will be expecting local authorities to consider this option in their business plans, and that they might lose out on government investment if they don't. This appears to be a return to the policy on stock transfer developed by the Conservatives in 1996, where local authorities are punished if they don't actively pursue the transfer route.

It therefore appears that the only way that local authorities can achieve private investment for their stock is through transferring either the ownership or the management of their stock to a private body. One way this might be done is by the use of the Private Finance Initiative.

Private Finance Initiative

The Private Finance Initiative (PFI) is another area of policy initiated by the Conservatives that has been developed and extended by the Blair administration. The PFI was originally introduced in 1992 to allow public bodies to develop capital projects using private finance and private developers and operators. It has been used increasingly in the National Health Service and for road-building. The importance of the PFI is precisely that the public body may borrow without its contributing to the body's capital spending or capping limit, so long as there is 'adequate risk transfer' to the private sector. However, the public body still retains ownership of the project.

The PFI can be seen as a form of leasing in that the private developer builds the project and manages it for a set period under contract for an agreed fee. Thus effectively capital projects are funded out of recurrent revenue income, rather than by a lump capital sum at the start of the project. Local authorities have been able to develop PFI projects since 1996. The government allowed revenue support for these projects of £2 million for 1996/7 and £30 million for 1997/8, but HRA housing was excluded from these changed accounting regulations.

However, in 1999 the Labour government allowed eight local authorities to undertake 'pathfinder' projects using the PFI to demolish and refurbish their own stock (*Inside Housing*, 12 November 1999). The projects involve appointing a long-term contractor to develop, manage and maintain the housing in return for an annual fee. The local authorities receive a subsidy from the DETR to help fund the projects. The aim is to evaluate these projects to determine whether the PFI is a suitable vehicle to use on a larger scale. The DETR is providing £160 million for these pathfinder schemes in 2001/2. An additional £300 million has been allocated for the following two years. In late 2000 the DETR invited new bids for PFI projects to use these additional resources.

Single capital pot

In 1998 the government announced its intention to reform local authority capital finance to create a single capital account, thus stopping the direct earmarking of resources to housing (DETR, 1998). The consultation paper suggests that the current separate annual capital guidelines for housing, education, transport, social services and other services should be amalgamated into a single pot based on a joint needs assessment/performance criteria basis. This approach appears consistent with the Blair government's so-called holistic or joined-up approach to public and social policy, which recognises that key problems such as social exclusion cross departmental and institutional boundaries. This measure came into force in April 2001.

The government argues that a single pot would have the following benefits:

- It would give greater autonomy to local authorities, presumably in terms of their mix of spending.
- It would increase local accountability.
- It would allow greater opportunity to mobilise resources to tackle cross-service issues.
- It would provide greater stability, with less year-on-year variation in allocation.

- It would mean that local authorities would take greater responsibility for allocating resources rather than being dependent on government allocations.

However, the possible creation of a single pot has caused some concern. In particular, there are two issues:

- The government is not proposing to reduce its regulatory role, and this finance will still have to follow central direction to a large extent.
- Housing capital expenditure is one of the largest capital pots, but not the highest political priority, and there is thus a danger of housing spending being reduced to fund extra expenditure on priority areas such as education. However, this is now less of an issue, as from 2001 the majority of local authority housing basic credit approvals have been converted into a major repairs allowance (see the discussion on resource accounting on p. 73).

For the first year of the single capital pot's operation (2001/2), the performance element of the capital allocation has been cut from 50 per cent to 5 per cent.

The issue of the single capital pot has been somewhat superseded by the publication of a further green paper on local authority finance in September 2000 (DETR, 2000b) suggesting that the government intends more fundamental reforms of local authority finance. The suggestions proposed include:

- the replacement of annual credit approvals with grants; and
- the abolition of permission to borrow, to be replaced by a debt ratio and a legal requirement to maintain a balanced budget.

These proposals are seen by the DETR as offering greater freedom and autonomy. But the green paper stresses how these changes would need to be meshed into the Best Value and Inspectorate structures and would offer the possibility of reducing government support more readily if any local authority were found to be underperforming.

ACTIVITY 4.5

Consider what capital finance could be used for, now that local authorities are not building new dwellings.

Housing revenue

Having examined the capital system, we now need to consider the revenue side. As I stated above, revenue generally refers to spending incurred in one year. However, loans for housing capital projects are repaid from the housing revenue account, and historically, debt charges have represented a significant element of revenue expenditure. Indeed, the purpose of central government subsidies was to cover the deficit between income and expenditure caused by borrowing for capital projects.

Over the past twenty years, but particularly since 1989, there has been a major shift in the relative importance of capital and revenue finance. Local authorities are not building new dwellings and are concentrating instead on the management and maintenance of their existing stock and the enabling of other social landlords to build to meet local housing need. This emphasis on management and maintenance puts a greater emphasis on revenue finance.

The change to resource accounting in 2001 will institutionalise this shift towards management and maintenance by creating a proper landlord account, and will force local authorities to make provision for repairs and maintenance. There is much speculation as to the effect that resource accounting will have. But the announcement in July 2000 that two-thirds of capital expenditure is to be converted to a major repairs allowance paid through the HRA indicates that resource accounting will further shift the balance towards revenue funding.

The aim of resource accounting is to make the value of a local authority's assets more transparent and to encourage it to plan in a more commercial manner. Garnett (2000) has suggested that it will make local authorities more like housing associations. What this implies is a blurring of the distinction between revenue and capital finance.

But resource accounting will also have one further effect: it will finally lay to rest the notion that local authorities are mass housebuilders. Resource accounting clearly prioritises the landlord function – management and maintenance – over any development role.

Resource accounting is clearly an important development, and one we will need to dwell on later in this chapter. However, before doing so, we need to understand some of the basic elements of the revenue finance system. Although resource accounting appears to be a new approach to local authority housing finance, these proposals will build on elements that have been in operation for nearly twenty years. Perhaps the most important mechanism is the notional HRA.

Notional housing revenue accounts

We have seen in Chapter 3 that governments since the mid-1970s have tried to exercise greater levels of control over local authority finance. In the early 1970s the Heath government attempted to use legal sanctions against recalcitrant councils (Malpass, 1990). This attempt failed because it was long-winded and politically divisive, as the controversy in Clay Cross proved. Clay Cross was a local authority in Derbyshire that refused to implement the rent increases demanded by the 1974 Act. After a long and bitter political struggle the Labour councillors were surcharged and debarred from office, and an administrator was brought in to implement central government's will. Accordingly, the Thatcher government attempted to use financial levers instead of legal sanctions. The Housing Act 1980 introduced an important innovation allowing the government to exert financial, rather than legal, pressure on local authorities. This mechanism was the notional HRA, in which the DoE determined reckonable income and reckonable expenditure. This was what each local authority *ought* to be spending in order to fulfil its obligations. These reckonable amounts might not, however, equate with what local authorities were spending or wanted to spend. The manipulation of these reckonable amounts (i.e. the relative increases of one in relation to the other) allowed government control over rents, largely by assuming that rents should rise faster than expenditure. The level of housing deficit subsidy was set according to the notional figures on the assumption that local authorities would follow them. Of course, the fact that subsidy was fixed meant that local authorities had to increase rents to achieve the desired level of spending. The only alternative to rent increases would be to reduce expenditure.

The effect of this mechanism, however, was that by the late 1980s most authorities had been removed from housing subsidy. This meant that central government lost its leverage over them. Government could influence rent levels only if they had to be used to offset falling subsidy levels. Once subsidy had fallen to zero, government could have no further influence over rents. This was remedied by the Local Government and Housing Act 1989, which brought all local authorities back into subsidy and introduced mechanisms giving government permanent control over the HRA even when subsidy is not paid. The key elements of the 1989 Act still form the basis for local authority revenue finance.

The Local Government and Housing Act 1989

The Local Government and Housing Act 1989 was introduced to remedy some of the problems of the system that had been in operation since 1980. These were:

- Government had lost leverage over most local authorities that were no longer receiving subsidy.
- But several of those in subsidy were actually operating at a surplus and transferring funds from the HRA to the General Fund.
- This ability to transfer between HRA and General Fund allowed local authorities to cross-subsidise and therefore, it was argued, hide management inefficiencies in their housing management systems. For instance, it was argued that some large urban authorities had unacceptably high rent arrears, which they need not deal with because they were subsidising rents from the General Fund. Other authorities used council rents – and hence housing benefit – to keep the rates down.
- The cost of rent rebates was growing, owing to the increase in the number of economically inactive tenants.

The 1989 Act was aimed at dealing with these problems and sought to regain central government control over the income and expenditure of local authorities. The Act retained the idea of the notional HRA, but now prescribed more tightly what could be included in it (Table 4.1).

Table 4.1 HRA under the Local Government and Housing Act 1989

Income	Expenditure
Gross rents	Repairs and maintenance
Service charges	Management
HRA subsidy	Revenue contributions to capital
Interest[a]	Rent rebates
	Loan charges
	Rents, etc. due by local authority

Note: [a] Interest on reserved portion of capital receipts as yet unused to pay off debt.

Ring fencing

The HRA was thus *ring-fenced*, and transfers out of the HRA to the General Fund may no longer be made as a matter of policy. A transfer may be made only if a local authority has a notional surplus greater than the actual cost of rent rebates (see p. 69). Indeed, the DETR may insist that this transfer is made. It is the power to force the transfer of notional surpluses that gave central government the continued control over a local authority's HRA even when no subsidy was being paid. The determination of a notional surplus, coupled with the requirement that an authority must balance its budget, allowed government continued leverage over rent and service levels. As part of resource accounting, the government is to allow authorities to retain surpluses so long as they use these for major repairs. This, of course, will allow government to minimise its future subsidy liability.

This ring-fencing mechanism is important in that:

- It encourages local authorities to maximise their rent income, as the only other source of income is subsidy.
- It acts as a spur to efficient management, particularly with regard to voids and rent arrears.
- By isolating housing expenditure, government could control it without its impacting on other areas of expenditure.

The Labour government's green paper on local government finance (DETR, 2000b) retains a commitment to keep the ring fence around the housing function. This is justified in that housing is funded out of rents and government subsidy for a minority of local taxpayers, whilst all other local authority services are funded through council tax and central government subsidies for the benefit of all taxpayers. Thus the green paper argues that cross-subsidies 'would be seen as inequitable to both council tenants and local taxpayers' (DETR, 2000b, p. 40). The government argues that resource accounting and business planning merely strengthen the case for the ring fence.

Central government subsidy

Under the revenue finance system in operation before the 1989 Act, the HRA could receive subsidy from three possible sources:

- *housing subsidy* to cover the notional deficit between reckonable income and expenditure in the HRA;
- *block grant* paid to the General Fund, but transferred into the HRA; and
- *rent rebate subsidy*, paid by the Department of Social Security (DSS) to cover the actual cost of rent rebates.

By introducing ring fencing, the 1989 Act ensured that cross-subsidies were no longer possible. This prevented block grant from being used in the HRA.

The other two subsidies were combined into a unified *HRA subsidy* paid by the DETR. This meant that rent rebate payments to council tenants were brought into the deficit subsidy system. The immediate consequence of this change was to bring all local authorities back into subsidy and thus give government leverage over spending and rent levels.

The other aim of this unification of subsidies was to limit central government's liability to fund rent rebates. The effect was to allow government to use notional surpluses in the HRA to help pay for rent rebates. This meant that those local authorities deemed to be in surplus did not receive a full refund for their housing benefit costs, as had been the case prior to the 1989 Act. To achieve this outcome, the two elements of the unified HRA subsidy – deficit subsidy and rent rebate subsidy – are in fact calculated *separately*.

Local authorities are able to reclaim 95 per cent of their actual housing benefit costs, including administration. However, the amount they actually receive is determined by the relative position of reckonable income and reckonable expenditure in the notional HRA. This is demonstrated in Table 4.2. Example 1 shows the situation of a local authority with a deficit on reckonable income and thus in need of deficit subsidy. This is added to the actual cost of rent rebates to give the total for HRA subsidy. However, in example 2 reckonable income exceeds reckonable expenditure and thus there is a notional surplus. This is used to reduce the amount of rent rebate subsidy paid to the authority.

The government was able to achieve its aim of controlling the level of subsidy by the manipulation of the main element of income (*rent*) and expenditure (*management and maintenance allowances*). The difference between these two elements of the HRA gives the housing element of the subsidy. If rent guidelines increase by more than allowances, then the level of subsidy can be reduced. This in fact occurred every year between

Table 4.2 *Operation of the HRA*

EXAMPLE 1: WHERE AUTHORITY IS IN NOTIONAL DEFICIT

(a) Reckonable expenditure (excluding rent rebates)	£11m
(b) Reckonable income (excluding subsidy)	£10m
(c) Therefore a notional deficit of	£1m
(d) Add rent rebates	£12.5m
(e) Therefore HRA subsidy (c + d)	£13.5m

Income (b + e) and expenditure (a + d) balance at £23.5m

EXAMPLE 2: WHERE AUTHORITY IS IN NOTIONAL SURPLUS

(a) Reckonable expenditure (excluding rent rebates)	£9m
(b) Reckonable income (excluding subsidy)	£10m
(c) Therefore a notional surplus (negative subsidy entitlement) of	£1m
(d) Add rent rebates	£12.5m
(e) Therefore HRA subsidy (c + d)	£11.5m

Income (b + e) and expenditure (a + d) balance at £21.5m

1990 and 1996. Indeed, it was clear that one of the main aims of this mechanism was to shift local authorities into the case demonstrated by example 2. In some cases the local authority's notional surplus was greater than the cost of rent rebates and thus no subsidy was paid at all. However, as the Secretary of State had the power to transfer the notional surplus to the General Fund in these cases, the government maintained leverage even when no subsidy was paid.

The government gave each local authority an annual *rent guideline increase*. The original aim in 1989 was to shift towards capital rents, whereby the rent charged mirrored the capital values of the dwellings, rather than the cost of provision. Thus there should be disparities in local rents akin to house price differentials across the country. Rent differentials were to be calculated on the basis of a comparison between an individual authority's capital values with the national average, using recent undiscounted right-to-buy valuations. This would give the relative value of a local authority's stock in relation to others.

However, the outcomes of this process were dampened to ensure that rises were not too large (and that rents were not reduced in some areas). Thus the government set minimum and maximum guideline increases and placed each local authority within these levels.

Rents set according to capital values were never achieved. As we shall see below, the actual operation of the system – which led to large rent increases – meant that the priorities with regard to rents were altered and the shift towards capital rents effectively abandoned (only to be resurrected again in the 2000 green paper).

Management and maintenance allowances were set initially on the basis of actual spending in the three years 1986/7 to 1988/9. In subsequent years the levels were determined by the relationship of an individual local authority's management and maintenance spending to the national average. Each authority was 'scored' and its allowances set accordingly. A score of 100 was the average and thus a score of 120 meant that the authority received 120 per cent of the national allowance. Again this system had to be dampened to ensure that the changes were not too drastic.

These guidelines and allowances were not binding on local authorities. They could choose to ignore the rent guideline and not increase rents, or they could decide to spend more on maintenance. However, the housing element of HRA subsidy was calculated on the assumption that these guidelines had been followed. Thus, if an authority wished to increase spending on management and maintenance, it might have to charge rents higher than the guideline increase. This was indeed what frequently occurred, and thus rent increases often outstripped the guidelines.

ACTIVITY 4.6

Referring back to Table 4.2, calculate the amount of subsidy where:

Reckonable income   = £17.5 million
Reckonable expenditure = £14.5 million
Rent rebates   = £18 million

The effects of the 1989 Act were dramatic. There are now only a minority of local authorities that receive their full rent rebate subsidy (as in example 1), and some have to cover all the costs themselves. In addition, since 1994/5 the housing element of the subsidy has effectively been negative, in that local authority contributions to rent rebates (negative subsidy entitlements) have been greater than the housing deficit subsidy (positive subsidy entitlements). The amount of the net surpluses (aggregate negative subsidy entitlements minus positive housing subsidy entitlements) for England is shown in Table 4.3.

What this means is that in 2000/1 rent surpluses are planned to contribute £1,508 million to the cost of rent rebates, which will only partially be

Table 4.3 *Growth of HRA net rent surpluses used to fund rent rebates*

Year	Surplus	Year	Surplus
1994/5	£108m	1998/9	£740m
1995/6	£408m	1999/2000	£884m
1996/7	£481m	2000/1	£1,015m[a]
1997/8	£563m	2001/2	£1,078m[a]

Source: Wilcox (2000)

Note: [a]Plans.

offset by £430 million paid out by government in subsidy. We can thus suggest that as net local authority contributions exceed housing subsidy, central government is effectively running council housing at a profit. Thus the routine management and maintenance of council housing does not cost central government anything.

The main argument against the policy is that it is inequitable, in that tenants in work are subsidising those on benefit. Hence it is frequently referred to as 'the tax on tenants'. As part of the resource accounting proposals, the government intends to remove rent rebates from the HRA. However, it still intends to 'capture' rent surpluses to offset the cost of rent rebates.

Controlling rents

The effect of this policy turned out to be somewhat self-defeating. Rents rose from an average of £19.01 in 1988/9 to £42.01 in 1998/9, which was well in excess of government guideline increases. The effect of these increased rents has been to increase the housing benefit liability, despite the contribution made by local authorities. Government may have been able to limit its liability, but it left a loophole that was to prove fatal to the attempt to operate capital rents.

The government's view was that housing benefit could 'take the strain' of the intended rent increases brought in by the post-1989 subsidy reductions. However, the new regime was introduced just as the economy went into recession, causing an increase in unemployment and hence in the number of benefit claimants. Thus by the mid-1990s, on average 66 per cent of council tenants were in receipt of housing benefit. This level of benefit dependency meant that any increase in rents would have a direct impact on housing benefit costs.

The loophole left by the Conservatives was to make the rent guideline only indicative and not compulsory. Whilst there was little benefit to an authority in raising rents below the guideline (except perhaps in an election year), there was a positive incentive to increase rents above the guideline. Indeed, as the number of benefit recipients rose, it became even easier, as fewer tenants were actually inconvenienced by the rent increases themselves. It is important to note here that local authority rent rebates are not paid from the government to the tenant who then pays his or her rent, but rather are paid direct to the local authority.

Local authorities argued that above-guideline increases were necessary because of the tight restrictions on management and maintenance allowances. Indeed, government did assume that these allowances needed to rise more slowly than income increased. Local authorities offered several justifications for higher expenditure on management and maintenance:

- Prior to 1990, many local authorities capitalised their repairs to take advantage of the availability of capital receipts. After ring fencing this was no longer possible, which therefore placed a greater burden on the HRA. The government partially recognised this problem, but allowed only a 3 per cent increase in allowances, whereas local authorities felt a 10 per cent increase would have been more realistic.
- As local authorities were no longer building, their stock was ageing, and thus maintenance costs would be expected to rise as a proportion of total costs.
- The worst-quality and hard-to-let properties are left as a result of the right to buy, leaving problem and hard-to-let properties to form a greater proportion of the stock.
- The use of decentralised housing management increased costs.
- The sale of a considerable portion of the stock under the right to buy has reduced total rent income, without reducing liabilities.

Although local authorities felt they could justify their large rent increases, the government chose to act to restrict rent increases. This was partly in response to a perceived affordability problem. But it was mainly due to the burgeoning housing benefit bill. The government therefore reversed its high rent policy and reverted to attempts to control rents.

Instead of an above-inflation rent increase, as had been typical between 1990 and 1996, the rent guideline increase for 1996/7 was put at zero, with management and maintenance allowances rising by less than 1 per cent. But the government also altered the rules regarding the payment of rent rebate subsidy to local authorities. From April 1996 authorities would receive rent rebate subsidy only at the rent guideline level. This means that as local authorities have around 66 per cent of tenants on housing benefit, there is little incentive for them to increase rents above the guideline. The alternative would be to increase rents by £3 for every £1 required, and thus the increase would fall exclusively on the third of tenants paying their own rent.

Since then, guideline rent increases have been lower than those in the early 1990s. For instance, the guideline increase for 1998/9 was 2.79 per cent, equating to a 96p increase on an average rent of £42.01. What is interesting is that whilst overall increases were within the government guidelines, some local authorities were prepared to impose a rent increase above the guideline level.

What this change in policy indicated was that the policy developed in the 1989 Act, of high rents and reducing subsidies, was unsustainable. Housing benefit could not take the strain and government has had to return to some form of rent controls, albeit without the statutory backing of the period between 1915 and

ACTIVITY 4.7

List the reasons why rents rose so much between 1989 and 1996. How could this have been avoided?

1989. The Blair government, after largely following the Conservatives' policies and spending plans for its first two years in office, has reacted to this unsustainability with an increase in expenditure and by a restructuring of both the HRA and rent policy.

Resource accounting

In December 1998 the DETR released a consultation document proposing major changes to the HRA. These changes are in recognition of the changing role of local authorities as managers and maintainers and not developers. Hence there will be a shift away from the recording of historic debt incurred in asset formation (the cost of housebuilding) in the HRA. Instead, local authorities are to record the current value of their assets. This means that each authority has to be aware of the condition of the stock and the amount needed to improve it.

Resource accounting can be seen as an attempt to 'measure on a consistent basis the resources used over the lifetime of houses, rather than simply the cash spent on them each year' (Malpass and Aughton, 1999, p. 34). Resource accounting came into operation in April 2001.

A further key aim of the New Financial Framework (as it has become known) is to make the system of housing finance more transparent to key stakeholders, particularly councillors and tenants. The intention is that councillors will be better able to take decisions on the use of councils' housing resources. Likewise, it is hoped that tenants will be better able to understand their council's policies.

Each local authority will have to produce a figure for the current value of its stock and each year the expenditure side of the HRA will have to show an amount equal to 6 per cent of that valuation. This means that each authority will have to generate a rate of return of 6 per cent on its housing assets. Thus instead of showing interest paid and debt repayments on the expenditure side, the HRA will have to show the cost of capital (the 6 per cent figure) and an allowance for major repairs. The valuation of the stock is a complex process, but is aimed at assisting in identifying also the state of the stock and thus establishing the true backlog of repairs needed to the housing stock.

The government intends that resource accounting will make local authorities more businesslike in their operation and will encourage them to manage their assets more effectively. Accordingly, they are expected to submit annual *HRA business plans* to the DETR beginning in 2001/2. These plans will indicate how the authority intends to use and enhance its assets over a period of up to thirty years. It is intended that in future business plans will mesh into the HIP system and the Best Value process. Thus the business plans will deal with future plans and how they are to be financed. Indeed, the political aim of business planning is to ensure that local authorities are clear about the nature and scale of the problems facing them and what options are available to them, such as stock transfer, establishing an arm's-length company or developing through the PFI.

The DETR aims to assist in this process by altering its annual capital allocations. Each local authority will now get a much lower level of BCAs, with the rest of the allocation now going to a *major repairs allowance* (MRA). The MRA is intended to deal with the maintenance of the council stock, whilst BCAs are to be used to improve the stock and deal with the backlog of repairs, calculated by the DETR as totalling £19 billion.

The initial DETR plans indicated a capital allocation for local authorities of £2,305 million for 2001/2. In July 2000 it was announced that only

£705 million of this would be in the form of BCAs, with £1,600 million going to the MRA. This equates to an average allowance of £559 per property, although the actual amount will differ according to the local condition of the stock. The government is committed to an inflation-linked increase to the amount per dwelling until 2004. However, the total cost of the MRA to the DETR is expected to decline. The Department's spending plans show a reduction to £1,512 million in 2002/3 and £1,403 million in 2003/4. BCAs will increase to £793 million and £842 million in each of these years. The reason for this overall decline despite maintaining the allowance per dwelling in real terms is that the DETR is expecting a reduction in the number of dwellings due to stock transfer. Importantly, as a revenue item the MRA will fall outside of the single capital pot, although, of course, BCAs will still be included in the single pot.

A further innovation is that a local authority will not necessarily have to spend all its MRA in one financial year. Dealing with certain major repairs is likely to take several years and the government believes that the funding mechanism should complement rather than detract from that. Moreover, HRA notional surpluses (once rent rebates are covered) will no longer have to be transferred into the General Fund, but can be retained. Of course, this will have the effect of limiting subsidy, as the HRA will balance with a lower MRA payment actually being made.

It is advised that the MRA is paid into a separate *housing repairs account*. Thus the amount used for major repairs will be transparent. The requirement for a separate account effectively ring-fences a dedicated amount to housing repairs, which cannot be used for other priorities even if the authority would wish to. A simplified HRA under resource accounting is shown in Table 4.4.

The consultation paper also proposed to remove rent rebates from the HRA and transfer them to the General Fund (which currently deals with private-sector payments). However, the government proposes that this change will not involve an increase in resources. Thus the DETR paper states, 'the government would still need to "capture" surplus rental income to offset the additional costs of funding rent rebates in full' (DETR, 1998, p. 11). The government argues that social housing is a 'national asset' and it is therefore right that 'assumed surpluses in authorities' housing accounts should be retained within housing and redistributed through a pooling mechanism' (DETR press release, 23 May 2000). This means that notional surpluses will be 'captured' by the DETR

Table 4.4 *HRA under resource accounting*

Income	Expenditure
Gross rents	Management and maintenance
Other income	Cost of capital[a]
HRA subsidy (inc. MRA and rent rebates[c])	Major repairs contribution[b]
	Rent rebates[c]
Other credits	Other debits

Notes:
[a] Six per cent of housing stock valuation.
[b] Transferred to housing repairs account.
[c] The intention is to remove rent rebates once primary legislation passes through Parliament.
HRA: housing revenue account; MRA: major repairs allowance

and used to offset the cost of housing benefit, even if those payments are to tenants of another authority. The changes to rent rebate need primary legislation, and, as yet, no date is set for when this change will be made. Therefore rent rebates will still appear on the expenditure side of the HRA and form part of HRA subsidy.

Resource accounting implies greater freedom to act in terms of target setting and planning. However, the use of measures such as business planning and the MRA, which are targeted and specific to each local authority, will give the Housing Inspectorate some measure of efficiency and allow for punitive measures against local authorities that are deemed not to be performing.

Rent restructuring

Whilst rent restructuring is likely to impact more on housing associations, in that their rents tend to be higher, it is important to consider the impact that it might have. The 2000 green paper suggests that the government's aim is to ensure that social rents are below market levels. In April 1999 the average council rent was £44 compared to £52 per week for housing associations and £75 for a private-sector assured rent. However, within these averages there are wide disparities, with some authorities charging higher rents than the housing associations in their area. Thus the government intends to restructure social rents over a ten-year period to ensure that there is comparability between the sectors. The relatively long restructuring period is intended to ensure that any changes are affordable. Thus no changes up or down are to be in excess of £2 per week.

Under rent restructuring, the rent guideline system is retained, but will be calculated differently. Rents will be determined according to a formula with 70 per cent based on local earnings and 30 per cent according to local capital values. The implications of rent restructuring will be dealt with more fully in Chapter 5.

Summary

In this chapter I have:

- considered the relationship between local and central government and stated that the balance since the 1970s has shifted decidedly in favour of the centre;

- explained the financial mechanisms controlling local authority capital expenditure;

- discussed the changes that have taken place to capital finance, particularly since 1997;

- explained the local authority revenue regime and looked at how central government has been able to manipulate expenditure through its subsidies arrangements;

- considered resource accounting and business planning and the intended impact these are likely to have; and

- shown the future prospects and problems facing local authorities.

Further reading

An important starting point is the 2000 green paper (DETR, 2000a), which outlines government thinking with regard to local authorities. Malpass (1990) discusses the history of subsidies, although without going beyond the introduction of the 1989 regime. However, Malpass et al. (1993) analyse the early implementation of the policy. Garnett (2000) offers a very detailed coverage of local authority housing finance, putting it in a more general local government finance context. Cole and Furbey (1994) offer a detailed critique of the politics issues surrounding council housing, concentrating particularly on its decline. Jenkins (1995) analyses the creeping centralisation of all aspects of public and social policy, including housing.

⑤ Housing associations

- The role of housing associations, particularly in relation to successive governments' housing policies
- The capital and revenue funding mechanisms
- The role played by private finance and the effect it has had on housing associations
- The implications for rent restructuring

Introduction

Even though housing associations have only 1.2 million properties (or 5 per cent of the total housing stock), they have been at the centre of housing policy since 1989. They are the main social landlords building new dwellings and accordingly have grown considerably, using a mix of public subsidy and private finance to fund new development. Housing associations have been central to the model of public provision developed by the Conservatives in the 1990s. This has involved the use of market disciplines within a framework of central government regulation and control. The expansion of housing associations has been funded by an injection of over £13 billion of private finance. Yet most associations still need public finance in order to develop and are, in consequence, regulated to ensure they fulfil the aims of government. Since 1989 government has reduced the level of public subsidy, requiring associations to increase the amount of private finance they must raise.

But there was a significant flaw in this policy. As the amount of public subsidy has declined, so have rents increased to repay the private loans. Initially, successive Conservative housing ministers argued that housing benefit could 'take the strain'. However, they underrated the strain that housing benefit would be placed under as housing associations increased rents to ensure their ability to meet their new long-term debts. Moreover, as rents rose, fewer households in low-paid employment could pay them, and as a result, housing associations became more dependent on housing benefit recipients.

The key problem in the housing association sector, therefore, is affordability. The 2000 housing green paper (DETR, 2000a) has addressed this problem by proposing the restructuring of rents in the social rented sector. The government proposes to restrict housing association rents to the rate of inflation plus 0.5 per cent from 2002, leaving associations only a very small increase in real terms in their main source of income. In addition, it is proposing measures to converge rent levels between housing associations and local authorities using a formula based on capital values (30 per cent) and disposable incomes (70 per cent). For many associations this will mean not only no increase in rents, but a decrease.

But many associations have taken on long-term loans to fund development on the assumption of real-term rent increases for years into the future. The fear is that some associations, particularly LSVT associations, may not be financially viable for long after 2002.

This is the context in which I want to discuss housing association finance. The period since 1989 has been one of significant growth, but at a cost, in terms of rents, that government now sees as unsustainable. But despite the increased use of private finance and the adoption of a more commercial outlook, associations are still threatened by a change in government policy. Housing associations, despite being private bodies and receiving less in the way of subsidy, are still dependent on government. The principal beneficiary of private finance was central government. However, when the benefit became less marked, it looked to reverse that policy.

Housing associations or registered social landlords

Since 1996 it has become common to refer to housing associations by the more general term of registered social landlord (RSL). However, as housing associations have a long history, a ready identity and a separate legal status, I shall persist in using their traditional name. Moreover, as probably 99 per cent of RSLs are housing associations, it is a rather unnecessary piece of jargon. If the government's plans for the transfer of local authority stock to new landlords become a reality (see Chapters 4, 9 and 10), then we may need to use an alternative term, but as yet it is unnecessary.

Are housing associations public or private bodies?

The first point to consider is just where housing associations fit in. In particular, are they part of the public sector or are they private bodies? Housing associations are either private limited companies or charities. In both cases they are managed by a committee or board of volunteers (hence housing associations used to be referred to as the voluntary housing movement). Prior to 1988, the majority of housing association committee members and staff would see themselves as fulfilling a function similar to that of local authorities, only on a smaller scale and perhaps, in many cases, through specialisation on certain types of need rather than by general provision. Associations were seen, and saw themselves, as welfare bodies, and this applied whether they were charities or companies. Of course, the relatively generous system of funding which operated up to 1989 helped to engender this view by cushioning associations from the realities of the commercial world.

However, the Housing Act 1988 designated housing associations as part of the *independent rented sector* along with private landlords. They were now to be seen as private-sector bodies, rather than as part of the public sector. Housing associations had now to fund their activities partly through private funds and had to ensure they had a sufficient income to meet their commitments. This income would have to come from rents and not from government subsidy. As a result, the ethos of housing associations has changed considerably.

But housing associations are still social landlords. They are still seen as performing a social function, even though they now supposedly bear the risk of commercial failure. Accordingly, they still receive government subsidy and are regulated to ensure that they meet the government's objectives. Therefore where do housing associations fit in? Table 5.1 summarises the situation.

Housing associations, then, are private bodies, but they build and manage housing according to publicly defined requirements and using public funding to assist them, all under a regulatory framework set by the government. In this regard they are rather similar to the privatised utilities such as gas, electricity and water. These types of organisations are defined as *parastatal*. They might not be state owned, but to all intents and purposes they are under public control.

The virtue for the government is that by using private bodies, it can transfer some of the responsibility and the risk, *but still maintain control*

Table 5.1 *Housing associations – public or private?*

Housing associations are:

- charitable trusts or private limited companies owned by shareholders;
- managed by board members who receive no payment but volunteer their expertise; and
- HA borrowing is private, not public, spending.

However, they also:

- receive government subsidy in the form of capital grants, whilst local authorities receive only permissions to borrow;
- are controlled by statute and are heavily regulated through the Housing Corporation, which has the ultimate power to disband the association and reassign its assets;
- have their rent levels determined by government; and
- own dwellings seen as public assets because they have been funded with public money.

over them. Housing associations, being private bodies, bear the risk of failure rather than government, even though failure might be largely due to the restrictions placed on them by government.

In any case, the reasons for placing housing associations at the centre of housing policy were not entirely positive. Associations were favoured not necessarily because of any special qualities they might possess, but rather because of what they were not. They were used as alternatives to local authorities, which were seen by the Conservatives as bureaucratic and unresponsive landlords (DoE, 1987). Housing associations, being present in most areas, were ready-placed vehicles allowing the government to bypass local authorities. This situation has not changed since the election of a Labour government in 1997. Whilst local authority spending has increased, associations are still the bodies entrusted with the limited level of new building deemed necessary.

It is important to note, however, that there is considerable diversity across the housing association movement. Associations range from large national associations with 30,000 properties to small, locally based associations with under ten dwellings. Also, because of the charitable nature of many

ACTIVITY 5.1

List the main differences between housing associations and local authorities.

associations, some specialise by concentrating on particular needs groups or types of accommodation. Other associations provide a full range of housing from supported schemes to large family housing. Some housing associations have more fully adopted the commercial disciplines of the 1990s and rely almost exclusively on private finance, whilst others are still dependent on subsidies. In short, therefore, there is no such thing as a typical housing association.

The role of government

Central government sets the parameters within which housing associations operate. It does this by:

- legislation;
- regulation and monitoring of standards; and
- funding.

However, unlike the situation with local authorities, government undertakes these procedures indirectly through a third party, the Housing Corporation. This is because associations are organisations legally independent of government.

But, in practice, because of their funding and the regulation that comes as a condition of that funding, they are very much dependent on government. Unlike local authorities, they have no sense of political legitimacy beyond their role as determined by government. Housing associations cannot claim an electoral mandate to be carrying out the settled will of the local populace. An association is a private charity or company *choosing* to provide subsidised housing and seeking government support in order to do so. Housing associations therefore have voluntarily acceded to government regulation as the price of subsidy. However, once it has accepted government subsidy, it is difficult for an association to break free from central control and regulation. It must accept subsidy on the government's terms, and that means sacrificing a considerable amount of autonomy.

The level of government support to housing associations is determined as much by the need to control public spending as it is by housing need. As with all areas of government spending, the control total for public spending is decided before allocations and priorities are set.

As with other areas of housing, it is not just a matter of total expenditure allocated to housing associations, but also the mechanisms through which the money may be used. Thus government in the early 1990s was able both to reduce the funding to housing associations in real terms *and* to increase the level of output. This was achieved by limiting the amount of public funding used to build each new dwelling. Associations had to make up the difference with private finance.

The pre-1988 system

Capital subsidies to housing associations were introduced only in 1974, in the form of housing association grant (HAG). This is now referred to as *residual or deficit HAG*. It aimed to enable associations to cover the costs of a scheme from its *first year's income*. Once a scheme was completed and a fair rent approved by the rent officer, the following formula was applied:

Annual fair rent	–	Maintenance and management allowances	–	4% voids	=	Amount available to service a residual loan

The annual amount available to service a loan was capitalised up to form a loan to be repaid to the Housing Corporation, which had already given the association the full cost of developing the scheme. The difference between this residual loan and the capital cost of the scheme was made up via HAG, thus:

HAG = Capital cost – Residual loan

This was an effective system, in that it allowed associations a degree of security, and the schemes they built were generally of high quality. However, the level of subsidy averaged between 75 and 90 per cent and could be as high as 100 per cent where allowances were greater than rent income. The system was also somewhat bureaucratic and complex to administer. In addition, housing association rents, being set by the independent rent officer, bore no real relationship to the cost of provision or of managing the scheme. Indeed, it was actually possible to get more than 100 per cent subsidy on some schemes. This was because of the availability of deficit revenue subsidies in cases where the income from the scheme did not meet allowable expenditure (see the discussion on the revenue funding system before 1989 below). Accordingly, the Conservative government, having been re-elected in 1987, set about reforming the housing association sector, with the aim of introducing risk to the development process. This policy was enacted in the Housing Act 1988.

Housing Act 1988

As was suggested above, government is able to control housing associations through legislation. Much of the current financing regime for housing associations is determined by the Housing Act 1988. In particular, it made three fundamental changes that affected housing association funding:

- There was a shift from secure tenancies with fair rents to assured tenancies with rents determined by contractual agreement between landlord and tenant rather than by the independent rent officer.
- Deficit revenue subsidies were removed, with the aim of introducing risk as an incentive to greater efficiency.
- Instead of grant being determined at the completion of a scheme, it is now predetermined, and thus associations have to raise the difference between the grant and the capital cost of development themselves using reserves, local authority support or private finance (or a combination of all three). The prevailing grant rate is the maximum amount of public subsidy that can be used in a scheme. This means that local authority support reduces the amount of grant.

There are several changes affecting rents and supported housing currently under way that will affect the financing of associations. However, the system introduced by the 1988 Act will largely remain intact. The rest of this chapter will consider how the system of housing association operates, beginning with the role of the Housing Corporation.

Role of the Housing Corporation

The Housing Corporation is the quango that funds, regulates, monitors and promotes the work of housing associations. It was founded in 1964 with a largely promotional role. It has been funded by government to subsidise housing association development since 1974. The Housing Corporation funds development through what is now called *social housing grant* (SHG), which replaced housing association grant in 1996.

The Housing Corporation is thus a powerful body, being able to exert considerable influence over housing association activities. This is particularly because housing associations are dependent on SHG in order to develop. This dependency has not been reduced as a result of the introduction of private finance. Very few associations have the ability to develop without recourse to subsidy, of which SHG is the main source.

The government gives an annual allocation to the Housing Corporation, and this is referred to as the *Approved Development Programme* (ADP). The ADP is the amount that the Housing Corporation has available to fund housing association activity in any one year. The ADP for 2000/1 was £637.2 million. The comprehensive spending review in July 2000 significantly increased the funding to the Housing Corporation, as follows:

2001/2	£995 million
2002/3	£1,158 million
2003/4	£1,460 million

This appears to be a significant increase in funding. However, this total in 2003/4 merely returns funding to the nominal level in 1994/5. Indeed, in 1992/3 the ADP was £2.3 billion.

The Housing Corporation allocates the ADP to its regional offices according to the Housing Needs Index (HNI). This is a series of indices aimed at comparing relative need down to the local authority level. The Housing Corporation is introducing a new allocation system between 2000 and 2004 which will take into account the different investment needs across the country. This is an attempt to deal with the problems of low-demand areas (i.e. where there is perhaps too much social housing), but also the needs of high-demand areas where new social housing is still needed.

Therefore from 2004 each local authority area will be guaranteed to receive no less than 80 per cent of its HNI. The remaining element will be determined according to the perceived investment needs of the area. In making these decisions three core objectives must be borne in mind:

- to provide new affordable housing according to local conditions;
- to regenerate the area by improvement or replacement of existing stock; and
- to contribute to the provision of new supported housing to meet the needs of vulnerable groups.

These objectives are central to two key documents in the investment process. First, each Housing Corporation region produces a *regional housing statement* in conjunction with the government regional office. This statement will span three to five years and is intended to provide an

> **ACTIVITY 5.2**
>
> What are the advantages of housing associations and local authorities co-ordinating development together?

overview of the priorities for the region in the light of the local economic and demographic circumstances. This statement is further supported by a *regional investment strategy* that highlights the priority areas for funding. It is this statement that forms the basis for individual bids from housing associations.

The bidding process

Individual housing associations are invited to bid annually for the next year's programme, normally by October. The bidding process is competitive in that associations are encouraged to bid for a fixed pot of money according to certain priority needs. These priorities are identified in the *regional investment strategy* published annually.

Housing association bids are currently judged on a competitive basis (i.e. average persons per dwelling, needs group, rehab or new build) according to the following criteria:

- Does it minimise the Housing Corporation's financial contribution? This is known as *grant stretch*, in that the use of private finance reduces the amount of social housing grant in any bid. Using accumulated reserves has the same effect.
- Does the proposed scheme satisfy housing need in terms of the design and quality of the scheme?
- Does the bid fall within the cost ceilings (see below)?
- Will rents be affordable to the intended client group?
- Does the bid meet the broader housing policy objectives such as helping to create sustainable communities?

In deciding between competing bids the Housing Corporation will take into account other factors such as the views of the relevant local authority and the track record of the housing association. The aim is to further integrate the ADP and HIP systems and to ensure that funding decisions by regional Housing Corporation offices are determined in relation to local authority business plans.

The total level of grant allocated to a scheme depends on two factors:

- *Total cost indicators* (TCIs) – these are cost limits for all the elements of the development process, aiming to ensure value for money. TCIs are set annually by the Housing Corporation and differ from region to region, taking into account regional cost differentials.

- *Grant rates* – the level of social housing grant allowed in each scheme is predetermined according to the type of scheme and location. In 1989/90 the grant rate was set at a national average of 75 per cent. This has been reduced over time and reached a low of 54 per cent in 1998. However, the grant rate for 2001/2 was increased to 60 per cent. The aim of this increase was to ensure that developments are affordable. This can be seen as a partial mitigation of the rent restructuring proposals due to be introduced in 2002. Predetermination means that cost overruns will not normally be covered by additional grant.

Social housing grant is paid in tranches according to the association's individual *cash planning target* (CPT). The CPT is effectively a forecast of when grant will be drawn down, and thus is aimed to create a degree of predictability in the development process.

The effect of the competitive bidding system is that it encourages housing associations to bid below the grant rate. This is because there are more bids than available funding. Thus, for example, even though the grant rate for 1998/9 was 54 per cent, the outcome of bids was grant at 50 per cent. This, of course, has made it more difficult for associations to claim that the grant rate isn't high enough. The ability of housing associations to operate with reducing grant rates might be explained by one of the following:

- The previous subsidy system was too generous and thus competition was forcing associations to make achievable efficiency savings.
- The fact that a majority of tenants were on housing benefit allowed associations to increase rents with relative impunity, knowing that increased rents would be covered by benefit.

Indeed, it is likely that the associations coped because of a combination of both these factors.

Effects of the capital system

The current system of housing association capital funding has had a number of effects:

- The aim of predetermined grants was to introduce an element of risk. Housing associations must bear the burden of any cost overruns in development and must ensure that they can meet their loan repayments from rent income. As a result, associations have undergone a considerable change in their cultures. They have shifted away from a welfare orientation towards a more commercial outlook.

- Housing associations have attempted to transfer risk to developers in the form of fixed price or *design and build contracts*. This is where the association engages a developer to build a scheme according to a design brief. The developer shares some of the risk because the contract price is fixed at the outset. This makes the development process more predictable for the association, but has meant less innovation in the design of schemes.
- The reduction in grant rates has created an increasing problem of affordability and burgeoning housing benefit costs. This issue will be discussed in detail in the following sections.
- The continued reduction in funding has led to some concern over the quality of new development.
- There is now much greater centralisation, with the sector being dominated by a few large national and regional housing associations that are able to build more quickly and cheaply, taking advantage of economies of scale.
- Since the mid-1990s there has been a much more interventionist attitude on the part of the Housing Corporation, particularly regarding the financial viability of housing associations. The attitude of the Housing Corporation appears to have been that associations must be commercially orientated to attract private finance. Much of the Housing Corporation's regulation is therefore geared towards ensuring financial viability by insisting on business plans, rent-setting policies, major repairs provisions and the proper presentation of accounts.

Housing association revenue

As intimated above, the operation of the capital system has revenue implications, particularly in relation to rents. Indeed, rent is the main source of revenue for housing associations. We therefore need to understand the various revenue mechanisms that operate. This will involve looking first at the revenue system that operated before the Housing Act 1988 was introduced. This is because the post-1988 system was built on what preceded it.

Revenue before 1989

Government subsidies to housing associations have predominantly been in the form of capital grants and residual loans. However, the framework established in 1974 also allowed the Housing Corporation to offer deficit subsidies for those schemes whose reckonable expenditure exceeded reckonable income. This was seen as necessary because rents were set not by the associations themselves, but by the independent county rent officer. It is important to realise that associations had to account for each scheme separately and this effectively prevented them from rent pooling.

The two revenue subsidies available to associations were:

- *Revenue deficit grant* (RDG), which was calculated on a scheme-by-scheme basis and covered the deficit between income and expenditure net of reasonable management and maintenance allowances and an assumption of 4 per cent voids. This was then aggregated across the association's schemes and RDG was paid where there was an overall deficit.
- *Hostel deficit grant* (HDG) operated in a similar way but pertained to special needs schemes and thus had a higher voids level (25 per cent) and assumed higher management and maintenance costs.

The operation of the post-1974 capital system meant that loan repayments to the Housing Corporation were fixed on scheme completion. This meant that as rents rose, associations quickly began to show a surplus on their general housing schemes. The government felt that this position had reached unreasonable proportions by the early 1980s and so introduced a means of clawing back surpluses from associations in the form of the *Grant Redemption Fund* (GRF). Associations were required to maintain such a fund and were obliged to place their surpluses in it according to the following formula:

$$GRF = Rent\ income - (M\ \&\ M\ allowances + Loan\ servicing)$$

If the sum of these amounts across all grant-funded schemes was positive (i.e. after clearing existing RDG entitlement), the surplus had to be placed in the GRF. It could be used for three purposes:

- for items of one-off expenditure approved by the Secretary of State;
- to offset future RDG entitlement; or
- taken back by the Housing Corporation.

Thus the post-1974 system had created a situation where some associations needed a revenue subsidy largely because they were not able to set their own rents. This was largely a stable system, in that it offered housing associations the security to develop. However, it did have a number of faults:

- Associations had an incentive to spend up to their management and maintenance allowances and thus to maximise their RDG entitlement.
- The operation of the RDG did not encourage associations to build up reserves.
- Rents, being set by the county rent officer, were not related to costs.

Furthermore, the Conservatives sought to limit their financial commitment, whilst also increasing output. As we have also seen above, they sought to pass on the risk of development to associations.

Revenue after 1988

The Housing Act 1988 attempted to deal with these problems. Associations were no longer able to offer secure tenancies after 15 January 1989, but had to offer assured tenancies. These tenancies were contractual rather than statutory and were aimed at shifting the balance in favour of landlords. Associations were able to set their own rents on assured tenancies and thus over time they have been able to control their income more directly.

Revenue deficit grant was phased out and housing associations were expected to refinance loss-making schemes. It was argued that as the number of assured tenancies increased after 1989 the financial position of these schemes could be expected to improve as associations charged rents more in line with their costs.

Hostel deficit grant was replaced initially by a hybrid system. *Special needs management allowance* was offered to mixed-funded supported housing schemes (i.e. those built after 1989 using a mix of public and private finance). *Transitional special needs management allowance* was offered for schemes funded by residual HAG. These two allowances were in effect grants which associations had to bid for from the Housing Corporation. The two forms of allowance have now been merged into a single mechanism called *supported housing management grant* (SHMG).

However, SHMG is due to be incorporated into the government's *Supporting People* mechanism in 2003. This is an attempt to co-ordinate the funding of supported housing by bringing together the disparate funds into a combined grant to the local authority to plan, commission and fund support services provided by other organisations. The Supporting People grant will be made up from:

- SHMG (and Scottish and Welsh equivalents);
- the element of housing benefit and income support paid for support services (wardens, etc.);
- probation accommodation grant; and
- other relevant local authority spending.

The issue here for housing associations is that they will lose direct control of a part of their revenue. This may still be used for the same purpose, but in future it will be allocated by a body that has to be aware of other competing priorities.

The Grant Redemption Fund has been replaced by the more accurately titled *Rent Surplus Fund* (RSF). This is calculated according to the same formula as the GRF and again *relates to deficit HAG-funded schemes only*. It differs from the GRF to the extent that associations may keep their surpluses rather than returning them to the Housing Corporation. The aim of the RSF is to build up a major repairs fund. However, it can be used only to fund major repairs on residual HAG-funded schemes.

Associations need only put an inflation-linked surplus into the RSF. This means they have been able to use above-inflation rent increases for other purposes. By rent pooling they have been able to build up reserves for future development. In turn these reserves can be used to develop new schemes and limit their requirement for both SHG and private finance.

Associations receive no subsidy for mixed-funded schemes, other than the possibility of SHMG for supported housing projects. Associations are expected to ensure that a provision for major repairs is costed into the scheme at the outset and thus should become part of the test of viability for any scheme. Associations tend to differ in when they start to build up their major repairs provision on mixed-funded schemes. Some do not start to build up a fund until five or ten years after completion on the assumption that only cyclical maintenance will be necessary. This allows initial rents to be lower in the hope that future rent surpluses can be used to build the fund. Others take the view that it is better to build up the fund quickly and thus start from year one.

The changes since 1989 mean that housing associations are now very reliant on rents as the main source of income. Indeed, rents are the primary source from which associations can repay debt incurred in the development process. We therefore need to consider these two issues – private finance and rents – in more detail.

Private finance

The basis of the housing association finance system since 1989 is private finance. In order for housing associations to develop, they need to raise the difference between the grant rate and the total cost of development from private institutions such as building societies and banks.

The feeling in 1988 was that associations would struggle to attract sufficient levels of private finance. This was because they were largely unknown to the financial markets and thus might not be seen as a good risk.

However, housing associations have generally found themselves able to attract sufficient levels of private finance, for the following reasons:

- Associations initially had to pay a premium in terms of a higher rate of interest to offset the perceived risk to the lender.
- The recession in the domestic and commercial property market in the early 1990s left a pool of underutilised funds. Therefore private finance institutions were more receptive than might have been the case in the mid-1980s.
- Government subsidies make lending to private institutions more secure in that government limits the level of risk and ensures that the value of the completed development is considerably greater than the loan.
- The Housing Corporation put a major effort into ensuring the viability of the post-1988 system, as the government's aims of limiting public spending whilst increasing output could not be met without a ready supply of private finance. Hence the Corporation altered its regulatory regime to ensure that associations became more commercially orientated.
- Lower interest rates in the 1990s have generally made borrowing more manageable.
- Housing associations have had no viable alternative and thus have had to make the system work.

Accordingly, associations have generally had no difficulty in raising all the private finance they have needed. In total over £13 billion worth of private finance has been raised.

The viability of using private finance in the long term depends on a number of factors:

• Government policy on issues such as grant rates, rent levels and housing benefit entitlement. The increase in the average grant rates to 60 per cent for 2001/2 will mean that associations have to borrow less, and the postponing of housing benefit reform (see Chapter 6) will also add security. Against that, though, the proposals for rent restructuring and limiting rent increases have caused concern about the ability of associations to repay their debts and to achieve their development targets.
• Expectations of changes in interest rates over the period of the loan. This is especially the case as many loans were initially on a low start basis, which made them more affordable in the early years, but they need rent increases to fund higher repayments towards the end of the period.
• The state of alternative markets, e.g. commercial and domestic property markets, which are both much larger and more established markets.

One concern that has been aired is that as the housing association private finance market is new and developing quickly, there are no parameters to the market. This means there is no real understanding of the true levels of risk and what are the limits for lending. Mechanisms for dealing with failing housing associations have been in place since 1996, but, as yet, these have not been needed.

Despite the doubts about private finance, though, it is clear that associations have flourished under the post-1989 regime. The stock of housing association dwellings in the UK has increased from 661,000 (or 2.8 per cent) in 1989 to 1,225,000 in 1998 (4.9 per cent). Associations have clearly been able to adapt to the more commercial environment enforced upon them after 1989. They have thus proved themselves able to cope with risk.

ACTIVITY 5.3

Discuss whether it matters if housing associations use public or private funding as long as new social housing is built.

However, just how much risk are associations prey to? They may have to ensure that they can repay debts incurred in development. But since 1989 they have been able to increase rents by a considerable amount and thus shield themselves to a certain extent from the risk of private finance. We therefore need to consider the issue of rents. We shall see that it is rents and not private finance that are causing the major fault line in housing association finance.

Rents

Rent is the main source of income for housing associations and indeed has grown in importance with the ending of general deficit subsidies as described on p. 90. Therefore, rent is their sole source for repaying private-sector loans (apart from the sale of assets). Accordingly, in 1988 it was felt that associations should have greater control over rents if they were to be attractive investment vehicles for financial institutions. Housing associations therefore can set their own rents on assured tenancies. Rents on secure tenancies are still set by the independent rent officer service, but these have kept pace with assured rents to the extent that by 1998 the average housing association fair rent was higher than the assured rent (£54.51 compared to £53.16; see Wilcox, 2000).

Since 1989, associations have been able to rent-pool and thus cross-subsidise schemes. This makes new schemes more viable, as associations are not dependent solely on the income stream from the scheme being developed. As discussed above, associations are required to place only an inflation-linked increase into their rent surplus fund. This means that they can increase their rents above inflation and gain the benefits of rent pooling.

In terms of rent setting, the situation is complicated by the fact that fair rents were not abolished but phased out on the termination of tenancies. An association must therefore operate two distinct rent policies:

- one for secure tenancies with fair rents (tenancies begun before 15 January 1989); and
- one for assured tenancies (those that commenced after 15 January 1989).

Associations are expected to have a rent-setting policy that is part of their long-term business plan. The Housing Corporation requires them to prepare a five-year business plan which covers their investment and development plans. A crucial means of achieving their plans is a secure income stream. Hence associations need to ensure that their income is sufficient to meet their immediate requirements and to provide security in the future.

According to the Housing Corporation, the key elements of a rent-setting policy should be:

- to ensure that the association can fulfil its obligations; and
- to ensure that rents are affordable.

However, there has been a marked reluctance on the part of both government and the Housing Corporation to give any clear definition of affordability. During the passage of the Housing Act 1988 it was suggested that affordable rents were those that:

- are affordable to those in low-paid employment; and
- do not exceed market rents.

Table 5.2 shows the increase in assured rents since 1989. It shows significant rent increases in the early 1990s, rising from 11.2 per cent of earnings in 1989 to 16.6 per cent in 1995. Studies from this period showed that some rents were above market levels and that, as a result, applicants were turning down housing association properties on grounds of affordability (Chaplin *et al.*, 1995). The indications were clear that rents were becoming unaffordable for those on low incomes. This can also be shown by the increase in housing association tenants in receipt of housing benefit from 53 per cent in 1989 to 73 per cent in 1998 (Wilcox, 2000).

Table 5.2 *HA rents as a percentage of average earnings, 1989–99*

Year	Weekly rent	Rents as a percentage of earnings
1989	24.50	11.2
1990	28.97	12.1
1991	33.93	13.3
1992	39.03	14.5
1993	44.87	16.3
1994	45.90	16.2
1995	48.42	16.6
1996	50.24	16.6
1997	51.40	16.3
1998	53.40	16.2
1999	53.84	16.0

Source: Wilcox (2000), p. 171

As a result of this situation, one of the main priorities of the government and the Housing Corporation has been to control rent levels. Accordingly, rent levels are now included in the bidding process. The rent formula imposed by the Housing Corporation currently insists upon inflation plus 1 per cent. Development bids may be turned down if housing associations do not stick to this formula. The proposed rents for any scheme are also considered as one of the criteria in determining bids to support through the ADP. The Housing Corporation has used a policy of 'naming and shaming' those associations it deemed to be charging excessive rents.

The downside to this is that, whilst it obviously makes rents more affordable (or no more unaffordable), there are concerns that it could lead to insufficient resources to fund future repairs as associations are less able to build up reserves. Indeed, many associations have developed their business plans on the basis of real-term rent increases in excess of 5 per cent per annum.

This regime is clearly putting pressure on housing associations. Reports in 1999 suggested that a third of associations failed to keep within the RPI + 1 per cent regime (*Housing Today*, 21 October 1999). The RPI + 1 per cent increase in 1998/9 would have meant a limit of 4.7 per cent. Whilst in England the average rent increase was only 3.8 per cent, a sizeable minority of housing associations increased rent by considerably more, the highest being an 18 per cent increase. With inflation at historically low levels – rent increases in 2000/1 were limited to below 2.1 per cent – these pressures would only increase. The increase in the average grant rate from 54 per cent to 60 per cent will relieve some of this pressure. However, an increase in the grant rate implies a reduction in the number of dwellings built as a result.

Rent restructuring

The proposals for rent restructuring announced in the 2000 housing green paper will create much greater pressure on housing associations than anything they have experienced at present. The green paper proposed that from 2002, rent increases in the sector will be restricted to the rate of inflation (RPI + 0 per cent). After consultation the government altered the formula to RPI plus 0.5 per cent (DETR, 2000c).

In addition to restricting rent increases, the government is seeking to achieve some comparability across all social landlords in a locality. The government argues that 'choice in social housing is distorted when rents differ for no good reason' (DETR, 2000a, p. 5). One of the aims of the policy therefore is to 'reduce unjustifiable differences between the rents set by local authorities and by registered social landlords' (ibid., p. 93). Housing association rents are on average 20 per cent higher than local authority rents and the government proposes that there should be some convergence. Moreover, rents should be set in both sectors according to the same principles. The green paper suggests that rents will be set using a combination of local property values and average local earnings.

The implication, therefore, is that some associations will have to reduce their rents. The government expects that this convergence will be achieved gradually, perhaps taking as long as a decade. This is to ensure that the changes in any one year are not too great. Accordingly, no change will exceed £2 per week. Each property will be given a target rent with 70 per cent based on local earnings and the remaining 30 per cent based on local property values. The formula is geared to take account of bedroom size (DETR, 2000d). The DETR envisages a ten-year implementation period for social landlords to achieve their target rents.

The effects of rent restructuring on housing associations are likely to be dramatic. Many associations have business plans predicated on real-term rent increases, some of them in excess of 5 per cent in real terms. As we have seen above, part of this increase was to help fund future development, and thus limit future debt, as well as to ensure that existing debts are covered. Rent restructuring is therefore likely to lead to a reduction in housing association development. But the repercussions are potentially even more serious in that some associations argue that they will quickly slide into bankruptcy. Less dramatically, rent restructuring will affect staffing levels, salary levels and service provision.

According to DETR-funded research, associations owning 63 per cent of the housing stock would be viable, whilst the rest would have to undertake corrective strategies (DETR, 2000e). The study implies that larger associations feel they are better able to cope, in that whilst the viable associations owned 63 per cent of the stock, they comprised only 42.5 per cent of the sample.

The government, however, appears to be set on making these changes and has refused to contemplate any more softening of the proposals. The impression one has is that the government believes housing associations have profited from the post-1989 system and have not in fact borne the level of risk intended. Indeed, the ability of associations to set their rents

> ### ACTIVITY 5.4
>
> Consider the reasons why housing association rents might be higher than local authority rents.

and use the housing benefit system has meant that they have merely passed the risk back to the government. The next few years promise to be interesting and will tell us whether housing associations are crying wolf (remember, they have argued against all reforms since 1989) or whether rent restructuring is genuinely unworkable.

Summary

In this chapter I have:

- discussed the nature of housing associations as private charities and companies, yet bodies that are heavily dependent on government subsidy;

- discussed the funding role of the Housing Corporation;

- explained the past and current systems for supporting housing association capital programmes;

- looked at the pressure imposed on associations by the capital funding regime;

- explained the revenue finance system;

- discussed the key role played by private finance; and

- considered the issue of rent levels and the possible implications of rent restructuring.

Further reading

Garnett (2000) provides a good discussion on housing association finance, particularly with regard to investment issues. CIPFA, the Chartered Institute of Public Finance and Accountancy, publishes a manual of housing finance, updated quarterly, which covers housing association finance extremely comprehensively. More generally, Cope (1999) offers a good overall discussion of housing associations, whilst Malpass (2000) is particularly good on the historical context.

⬤ 6 ▸ The private rented sector

- ◉ The decline in private renting, largely due to differential treatment relative to the other housing tenures
- ◉ The relative lack of state subsidies to the private rented sector
- ◉ The various attempts made to revive the sector, particularly those since 1989
- ◉ The effects of deregulation since 1989, particularly with regard to rents and housing benefits
- ◉ The future direction of the sector

Introduction

The private rented sector in some ways can be seen as the Cinderella tenure, in that it has been neglected by government in terms of subsidies and protection. Successive governments have concentrated on social housing and owner occupation and ignored the needs of the private rented sector. However, other commentators, such as Albon and Stafford (1987), would suggest that the problem for private renting was not so much that it was neglected, but that it has been regulated in a particularly perverse way.

Whilst owner occupation and social housing have been developed by positive regulation and financial support, intervention in the private rented sector has had a rather more negative effect. Instead of subsidies coming from government, for much of the past century it was landlords subsidising their tenants through the imposition of rent controls. This meant that tenants have benefited at the expense of landlords. Not surprisingly, this led to a decline in private renting from the position where it was enjoyed by 89 per cent of households in 1915.

The issue here is not just the perverse nature of the subsidy, but the fact that the sector has suffered from a lack of support *relative* to other tenures. Whilst private landlords were subsidising the rents of their own tenants, local authorities, and later housing associations, were in receipt of government subsidies that benefited landlords and allowed them to pass this on to tenants in cheaper rents.

One of the aims of this chapter is to look at the decline in this sector and subsequent attempts to reform it to make it more sustainable. It is important to realise that this issue is not just quantitative, but also relates to the quality of housing in the sector. The problem is not just that the sector has contracted to a tenth of its size a hundred years ago, but that it is very much perceived as offering the poorest-quality dwellings, often to vulnerable groups such as young single persons, the homeless, minority ethnic groups and recent immigrants.

The introduction of rent allowances for private-sector tenants in 1972 and 1974, which are now incorporated into the housing benefit system, considerably altered the adverse position enjoyed by the private rented sector. Government subsidies now directly supported tenants, which in turn benefited landlords in that their rent income was secured to a much greater extent. However, this set of financial arrangements has not been without its problems. The support offered by the housing benefit system allowed landlords to increase rents without its directly impacting on tenants. This became more manifest with the phased removal of rent control following the Housing Act 1988. The Conservative government might have intended rents to rise as a means of encouraging landlords to remain in and expand the sector, but it had no effective means of controlling these rent rises. Since the mid-1990s there has also been considerable disquiet about the level of housing benefit fraud within the sector. Thus the concern for the private rented sector has shifted from concern at its decline to concern with the control of subsidies. In many ways, therefore, the same concerns which have dominated social housing now loom large over the private rented sector. This has meant that the liberalisation of the private rented sector has been only partial, with a distinct reversal of policy in the 1990s back towards the regulation of rents.

The 2000 housing green paper (DETR, 2000a) has made some attempt to deal with these problems by discussing possible changes to the eligibility for housing benefit in certain cases and the possibility of housing associations and other registered social landlords (RSLs) acting as managing agents to support private landlords. However, the green paper does not envisage any major changes to the private rented sector. This suggests that there is to be no determined attempt on the part of government to reverse the long-term decline of the tenure. Whilst the green paper proposes a significant increase in the transfer of local authority stock to private bodies, this is likely to benefit new or already established RSLs rather than private landlords as such. However, if this

ACTIVITY 6.1

What are the words that you most associate with the private rented sector?

proposal for the mass transfer of local authority housing does take place, it will necessitate a complete overhaul in the relations between social and private rented sectors and perhaps create a much more fluid and dynamic interaction between what has hitherto been a rather rigid divide between social and private rented sectors. This, though, is speculation about the future. What we need to do first is look at the various types of private landlord and then explore how private renting has got into the state it has.

Who are private landlords?

Despite the image of private renting, there is no such thing as a typical private landlord. They range from large commercial companies through to households who take in a lodger to help pay the bills.

Bevan *et al.* (1995) in their study on private landlords and housing benefit categorise private landlords into the following groups:

- *Sideline landlords*, for whom this is not their main business. They subdivide this category into *informal*, who see themselves as merely helping family and friends, and *formal* sideline landlords who have a more organised approach to letting and may have several properties.
- *Business landlords*, who have a number of properties and manage them as their full-time profession.
- *Managing agents*, who perform a complete lettings and management service on behalf of landlords. These agents may carry out this service for landlords who have only one or only a few properties and who may not have the time or expertise to manage the properties themselves.

Private landlords therefore tend to operate on a small scale, with only a minority operating on a commercial basis. This means that they are more susceptible to changes in market conditions, as they are less able to spread the risk over a large asset base.

Decline of the private rented sector

Prior to the First World War the private rented sector was the majority tenure, with 89 per cent of households (Table 6.1), compared to 10 per

Table 6.1 Decline of private renting in the UK

Year	Percentage of households renting from private landlords
1914	89
1945	62
1951	53
1961	31
1971	18.9
1981	11.1
1991	9.6
1998	10.6

Sources: Malpass and Murie (1999); Wilcox (2000)

cent in owner occupation and 1 per cent in local authority housing. As a tenure it could, then, be said to have been enjoyed by all social classes and to have provided for a range of needs. But this did not mean that all households were well housed. As we saw in Chapter 3, the period before the First World War was one of little government regulation of housing markets. Whilst markets might work well for those who have a secure income, they can guarantee little for those who haven't. Those on very low incomes might be able to find accommodation, but not of a quality deemed to be acceptable. Thus the problem with the private rented sector (and it is still the case now) is matching up quality and affordability. How can we ensure that there is a sufficient quantity of good-quality housing at affordable rents? The problem for private renting was that for much of the past century governments chose to use other tenures to solve the problem.

One can point to two further problems that affected the prospects for the private rented sector in the nineteenth and early twentieth centuries. First, the supply of housing tended to lag behind demand. The supply of housing is what economists term *inelastic*, by which they mean it is not flexible enough to respond quickly to changes in demand. One of the characteristics of housing is that it takes time to build, and this can be a particular problem if the increased demand is in an already built-up area. The effect of supply inelasticity is that when there is a change in demand, the price changes rather than quantity. This increase in rents might encourage landlords to build more dwellings, but they might also choose to wait to see whether the increase in demand is permanent, and they might also have difficulty in finding suitable land (which is likely to be expensive precisely because it is scarce). What was common throughout the nineteenth century was the division of dwellings into ever smaller units, allowing landlords to meet demand, but at the expense of overcrowding (Burnett, 1986).

The second problem is related, in that there was little in the way of controls over standards, be it in terms of overcrowding, sanitation or building regulations. Local authorities had been granted some permissive powers in the nineteenth century, but they were seldom given a duty to act. Even where a duty existed, they had little in the way of financial incentives to fulfil these responsibilities. Various charitable bodies had attempted to raise the standard of dwellings by developing so-called *model dwellings* to show that it was possible to make a reasonable rate of return on working-class housing. However, these 5 per cent philanthropists (so called because of the rate of return on investments they promised) failed to prompt a sufficient level of investment. There was also a feeling that the imposition of standards would merely raise the rents and only increase the problem of unaffordability. These three problems – of quality, quantity and affordability – therefore tended to grate together and present a problem which landlords themselves either could not or would not deal with. The scale of the problem was generally recognised and periodically became a public scandal, but it was only Britain's involvement in the First World War which forced government to directly intervene in the sector.

As we saw in Chapter 3, the war increased the demand for rented housing, yet prevented an increase in supply. More workers were needed for war manufacture, yet resources were needed for the war effort and could not be spared for housebuilding. The result was an increase in price. This was seen as profiteering and led to rent strikes across the country, but particularly in Glasgow in 1915 (Damer, 1992). The government responded to this with the Increase of Rent and Mortgage Interest (War Restrictions) Act 1915, which imposed a ceiling on rents and mortgage interest at their August 1914 levels. As the name of the measure suggests, this was intended as being temporary for the duration of the war, but in fact statutory rent controls existed in some form between 1915 and 1957, and between 1965 and 1989.

The effect of rent control was drastically to reduce the incentive to supply because landlords were not able to adjust their rents in line with changes in their expenditure. However, it also had the effect of increasing demand because dwellings were let at a cheaper rent than would be set in a free market and thus they were more affordable. This problem of excess demand would ordinarily have been met by an increase in rents, which in turn would have acted as a signal to increase supply. But rent controls not only prevented these market signals from operating, but actually created the opposite effect. Rents, of course, did not rise, which was of benefit to tenants. But landlords had a reduced incentive to invest in their properties because they could not secure a reasonable return on them. There was thus a reduction in the quality of dwellings as repairs and improvements were postponed. In addition, many landlords left the sector, often by selling to the sitting tenant.

The principal problem of rent control was that, unlike later forms of subsidy offered to owner occupiers and social landlords, it directly benefited one party – the tenant – at the expense of the other – the landlord. The government did not provide the subsidy, as it did in the case of subsidies to social landlords, but rather forced landlords to subsidise tenants by debarring them from increasing their rents. One need not have any particular sympathy towards private landlords to realise that this form of subsidy would act as a disincentive to them.

It was not possible to repeal rent controls in the immediate post-war period as the same conditions still pertained as had been the case in 1915. The demobilisation of the armies in Europe led to an increase in the demand for housing. Therefore rent controls remained after 1919.

Several attempts were made to abolish rent control, particularly by Conservative governments. The first was made in the mid-1930s, when controls were slowly lifted. But the advent of the Second World War in 1939 saw them reimposed. The next attempt came in the Rent Act 1957, which abolished all rent controls on properties with a high rateable value with immediate effect and decontrolled others on change of tenancy. The proponents of this measure argued that it would lead to a reversal of the decline in private renting. The Act's critics argued that rents would increase dramatically, standards would decline and harassment by landlords would be encouraged.

The Act's critics were indeed correct on the last two points. It was subsequent to the 1957 Act that the term *Rachmanism* was coined to refer to unscrupulous landlords (after the London landlord Peter Rachman) who harassed their tenants and made little attempt to maintain dwellings to a reasonable standard. However, rents did not rise dramatically. The reason for this was that local authority accommodation now formed a ready alternative to private renting. Indeed, in terms of quality, it was clearly superior, and thus private landlords found they could compete only in terms of rent levels. Government subsidies to local authorities enabled them to keep rents well below market rents and thus private landlords had to follow suit. The housing minister at the time, Enoch Powell, had wanted to deregulate council rents as well, so that the two sectors could compete properly, but he was overruled by the Prime Minister, Harold Macmillan.

The most noticeable effect of the Act, however, was to precipitate an increase in the rate of decline (Daunton, 1987). Landlords, who had no confidence that rent controls would not be reintroduced sometime in the future, took the enhanced opportunity to leave the sector. The Labour Party was committed to reintroducing rent controls, which it duly did in 1965. But also the lack of any positive encouragement to private landlords, beyond the ability to raise rents, meant that they had little incentive to increase their investments.

Perhaps the most lasting effect of this period, though, was the tarnishing of the image of private landlords as an exploitative class providing poor-quality housing. The view of private landlords as exploitative and venal, brought about by the activities of landlords such as Rachman, has never been lost. This perception has merely added to the already less appealing nature of private renting relative to social housing and owner occupation.

Unexpected consequences

What this episode also shows is that there are always unexpected consequences in housing policy (King, 1998). No one could have foreseen that the 1957 Act would have the reverse effect of that intended: that instead of rejuvenating the private rented sector, it actually hastened its decline and further tarnished the image of private landlords. Indeed, the whole history of rent controls in the private rented sector is evidence of the impact of the unforeseen on policy. What seemed to be sound and reasonable policies at the time, be it rent control or subsidies to local authorities, had the effect of reducing the one-time majority tenure to a rather neglected rump.

Governments, of course, when planning their policies, try to learn from the unexpected outcomes of previous policies. This was certainly the case with the next major attempt to repeal rent controls, that undertaken by the Thatcher government in the later 1980s. Instead of controls for some properties being withdrawn immediately, they were withdrawn at the change of tenancy. In addition, the Housing Act 1988 included enhanced measures for dealing with harassment by landlords. Thus it was hoped that abolition would not have the same dramatic effect and that a more sustainable position could be created.

However, the situation in this sector in 1989 (when the Act came into force) was markedly different from that in 1957. First, the sector was much smaller. In the late 1950s, nearly half of Britain's households were in private rented housing, whereas in 1989 the figure was only 8 per cent. This meant that the tenure was less significant politically and electorally. Second, the image of private landlords was such that they were not deemed especially deserving of support (even though this image, as Bevan *et al.* (1995) show, might represent a crude caricature of actual landlords). These two issues compounded each other to make private renting a lower priority than owner occupation in particular. This lack of support is evident even with the Conservatives in the later 1980s, and this is despite their rhetorical support as shown in the 1987 white paper *Housing: The Government's Proposals* (DoE, 1987).

The third change, though, is perhaps the most significant. By 1989 there was a comprehensive rent allowance system supporting the private rented sector. This had the effect of cushioning rent increases, meaning that tenants would not directly be affected by rent increases (unless, of course, their circumstances changed). When this is added to the enhanced anti-harassment measures in the 1988 Act one can see that tenants were much better protected in the late 1980s than in the later 1950s.

I shall deal with the housing benefit system in more detail in Chapter 8, but it is important to understand the impact that housing benefit has had on the private rented sector; in particular, how it has affected the Conservative government's attempted liberalisation of the tenure.

As in 1957, the critics of liberalisation in the private rented sector argued that rents would rise and the rights of tenants would be adversely affected. It was argued that the introduction of assured shorthold tenancies, whereby tenancies were time limited to a minimum of six months, would create greater insecurity and enforced mobility in the sector. This has occurred to an extent, particularly at the lower end of the market (but this was always the most volatile, as it tends to attract students and other young people who tend to be transient in an area). Indeed, the use of six-month assured shorthold tenancies quickly became the standard for the sector, as it gave landlords greater flexibility.

The critics of the 1988 Act have clearly been proved correct about rent levels. Indeed, one could suggest that the Conservative government intended rents to rise as a means of encouraging increased supply. However, it was not the operation of free markets that allowed landlords to raise rents, but rather the operation of the housing benefit system, which paid the actual rent to eligible claimants. This meant that rents could rise and tenants would not be directly affected. As a result, average

ACTIVITY 6.2

What are the attractions of the private rented sector?
Who might the tenure appeal to now?

rents for the sector rose from £24.00 in 1988 to figures in 1998 of £59.24 for a fair rent and £72.01 for a market rent (Wilcox, 2000).

New controls for old

What one could argue, therefore, is that whilst landlords might have suffered disproportionately from rent control, tenants have been protected from the main effects of the abolition of controls by the housing benefit system. On balance this would suggest that the policy had been implemented in a sensitive way, which would encourage new investment, or at least maintain the current level, without dramatically worsening the lot of the majority of tenants. The result was that the private rented sector began to make a slow recovery. (However, as we shall see in Chapter 8, the result of higher rents has been to increase the poverty trap, whereby many households are better off on benefits than in work.)

The problem, however, was that central government did not consider the situation a sustainable one. Rent controls were a policy measure which did not directly affect government expenditure, in that landlords paid the cost of subsidy. Yet the comprehensive nature of the housing benefit system has meant that the abolition of controls considerably increased government expenditure. Throughout the 1980s, housing benefit grew at the rate of 4 per cent a year. In the 1990s it grew at 11 per cent a year (DSS, 1997). However, the increase for the private rented sector (and housing associations, which are treated as private-sector landlords for the administration of housing benefit) was much larger:

> The rise in housing benefit expenditure for private and housing association tenants has been faster than for council tenants.
> Expenditure on benefit for private and housing association tenants has risen by an average of 20 per cent per year in real terms since 1990/91, compared with an average of 6 per cent in expenditure on benefit for council tenants.
>
> (DSS, 1997, p. 2)

The effect of this rate of increase is that whilst the private sector and housing associations made up only roughly a quarter of the cost of housing benefit in 1988, by 2000 it was forecast by the Department of Social Security that they would be taking nearly two-thirds of the total (DSS, 1997).

These trends in expenditure have led government to alter the benefit system to limit the effects of rent increases. As we shall see in Chapter 8, housing benefit has been restricted in all tenures, but it is only in the private rented sector that eligibility has been reduced. In the social housing sector administrative restrictions have been applied, but the eligibility restrictions to the under-25s and the local reference rent system do not apply.

Before we look at these measures, it is interesting to speculate on why there is this differential treatment. When the local reference rent system was mooted in the mid-1990s, originally it was to apply to the independent rented sector and thus the whole rent allowance system including housing associations. Local authorities were exempt because of their 'social' function, in that they were providing housing on the basis of need. This was despite the fact that local authority rents increased by an average of 36 per cent in real terms between 1990 and 1996, compared to an increase in the independent rented sector of 26 per cent between 1992 and 1996 (DSS, 1997; data for rent allowances were not collected before 1992).

However, as we have seen, the case for including housing associations in the local reference rent system was a strong one. Indeed, the DSS implies that the large increase in housing benefit costs in the independent rented sector was as much due to the growth in the housing association sector as to rent increases by private landlords. The number of housing association tenants in receipt of benefit has proportionally doubled, whilst the number in the private sector has stayed roughly stable (DSS, 1997). As a result, housing associations were able to argue that they too were fulfilling the same 'social' function as local authorities. Accordingly, the application of local reference rents to housing associations was made discretionary on the part of the relevant local authority administering the benefit locally. This has meant that the majority of housing associations are exempt from local reference rents.

It could be argued that social housing organisations operate on the basis of need, whilst private landlords operate on the basis of profit. As a result, there needs to be some regulation of private landlords to ensure that they do not unreasonably profiteer from tenants and, indirectly, the state. However, as Bevan *et al.* (1995) have shown, there are many reasons why people become private landlords. Many individuals, particularly in the early 1990s, took in lodgers to help meet their mortgage costs, or rented out a property they couldn't sell. Indeed, Bevan *et al.* (1995) suggest that these small-scale landlords, who have only a limited knowledge of housing benefit regulations, form a considerable part of the market. This was confirmed by DETR research which showed that only 49 per cent of personal landlords (those private individuals who personally manage their properties) were aware of the changes introduced in 1996 and only 34 per cent could explain what they were (DETR, 1999).

But whether landlords profiteer or not, is there any difference between the tenants who are housed by social and by private landlords? One can presume that households rent from private landlords in order to fulfil their housing need, just as social housing tenants do from their landlord. In this case, is there any justification for differential treatment of households who are otherwise similar merely because of their landlord? Why should 20-year-olds receive full housing benefit if they are in a housing association flat, but not if they rent from a private landlord? The distinction appears to be solely on the basis of presumptions about the landlord and not on the need of the tenant. This is particularly perverse as housing benefit is intended to help individuals to fulfil their needs. We shall consider the issue of entitlement to benefit in more detail in Chapter 8.

But whatever the reasoning, a series of restrictions were imposed on the private rented sector in 1996. In January 1996 the local reference rent (LRR) system was introduced. The LRR is the average rent for a particular property type in a particular area. The purpose of this change was to try to halt the increase in rents or even to decrease them by altering the incentives that operated in the housing benefit system. Instead of private-sector tenants receiving the full rent charged by the landlord, they would now receive payments up to a maximum determined by what is considered to be an appropriate level for the household and the LRR. This means that the size and composition of the household are taken into account to ensure that households are not underoccupying dwellings, but are living in properties that are appropriate for their needs. This was an attempt to deal with so-called 'upmarketing', where households would move to larger accommodation funded through the open-ended housing benefit system. Therefore one can say that the housing benefit system, at least insofar as the private sector is concerned, is no longer open ended.

When the system was introduced in 1996, claimants could receive half of the difference between the actual rent and the LRR. However, as from October 1997, claimants receive only the appropriate rent determined by their circumstances and the LRR.

The intention of this policy was to 'encourage' landlords to reduce their rents to what was considered an appropriate level. It would also ensure that tenants did not underoccupy large and expensive dwellings. As Bevan *et al.* (1995) suggest, the idea appeared to be that landlord and tenant would renegotiate their contract in the light of these changed circumstances. However, as critics of this measure were quick to point out, this 'renegotiation' depended upon an equal relationship between landlord and tenant. In particular, it implied that there was a ready supply of accommodation so that if a tenant, say, received only £50 per week, yet their landlord wanted to charge £60, there was alternative accommodation at £50 available. If this were not the case, it might be that tenants would have to find the difference between their housing benefit payment and the actual rent out of their income support.

Further changes limiting housing benefit payments for single persons under 25 were introduced in October 1996. The so-called 'single room rent' (SRR) measure limited benefit to the amount equivalent to the rent charged for shared accommodation. This meant that tenants under 25 would have to move to shared accommodation or fund the difference themselves. As with the LRR system, the under-25s rule applied only in the private rented sector. The government also changed the rules for the payment of housing benefit in October 1996, after which all new claims were paid wholly in arrears on a monthly basis. This meant, of course, that tenants would be permanently in arrears unless they could find a month's rent from other sources.

An area of concern for the Labour government which came to power in 1997 was the large increases being imposed on secure tenants with fair rents. This was where the tenancy pre-dated 15 January 1989 and was thus still covered by statutory rent controls. However, these increases, which impacted disproportionately on the elderly, were increasingly seen as excessive. Landlords were attempting to ensure that fair rents caught up with assured rents. In addition, as rents could be increased only every second year, increases were considerable. Therefore, in February 1999 the government limited the next fair rent increase to inflation plus 7.5 per cent and subsequent increases to 5 per cent over inflation. Unfortunately the government gave over six months' warning of this change and consequently some landlords tried to impose huge increases before the regulation came into force. These regulations have been placed into question by a successful legal challenge from a private landlord who argued that the government had no grounds to impose a rent cap.

Research published by the DETR (1999) analysed the effects of the changes made in 1996. It found that the behaviour of some landlords had changed. Some had refused to let to housing benefit claimants at all, others had dropped their standards and others were using tenants' deposits to clear arrears and thus not having to reduce rents. Likewise, some landlords operated differential lettings policies when letting to people under 25. Some would not let to that group at all, whilst others would let only certain types of property to this group.

The research found that few tenants had persuaded their landlord to reduce the rent, either before taking the tenancy or during its course. Landlords were reluctant to do so, arguing that it was the responsibility of tenants to pay their rent. It found that tenants would meet the shortfall in housing benefit either out of their income or by borrowing. The report, therefore, could offer little evidence that rents had fallen as a result of these measures.

However, Wilcox (1999) suggests that the private rented sector declined for the first time since the deregulation of the sector in 1989. He attributes this decline to 'the restrictions on private rents eligible for housing benefit introduced at the beginning of 1996' (p. 72). Between May 1997 and May 1998 there was a reduction of 100,000 private tenants claiming housing benefit, 'and most of that fall can be attributed to the benefit restrictions' (p. 72). However, he does suggest that the 'non-housing benefit' sub-sector of private renting continues to grow.

Despite the phasing out of statutory rent control from 1989, therefore, it is clear that some form of *administrative rent control* has been reintroduced, whereby government again is able to exert some downward pressure on rents. There is no intention on the part of the Labour government to reintroduce statutory controls (DETR, 2000a), but it is also certain that the Blair government, like its predecessor, is not prepared to let rents find their own level. This means that competition in the sector is seriously hampered as landlords, in effect, must charge a standard rent.

The private rented sector compared to other tenures

I have already suggested that one of the key reasons for the decline in the private rented sector has been the subsidisation of other sectors. Local authorities have received subsidies to provide new dwellings at cheap rents which were obviously more attractive than the private sector. Likewise, owner occupation has received more favourable treatment to the extent that it is often cheaper to pay a mortgage than to rent privately.

This is ironic in that many households during the recession in the early 1990s were forced into the private rented sector following the repossession of their dwelling, only to find themselves paying more a month than their mortgage. The difference for these households is that they could claim state support for rent payments, but not for mortgage repayments.

But private landlords receive little in the way of direct subsidy. Indeed, as we have seen, one of the key problems is that they have been directly subsidising tenants. In addition, unlike the tax exemptions enjoyed by owner occupiers and social landlords, the rent income of private landlords is taxable, although interest on investments is tax deductible. Moreover, private landlords receive no depreciation allowance as other businesses do, allowing them to offset the cost of eventual replacement against tax. That said, private landlords have in the past had access to improvement grants.

ACTIVITY 6.3

Compare the financial subsidies offered to the private rented sector with those offered to social housing. Give reasons for the differential treatment between the two rented sectors.

The problem for private renting is that it is politically insignificant compared to owner occupation and social housing. Owner occupation is the dominant tenure and this is what politicians tend to concentrate on. For many on the left, private renting is still anathema – housing for profit, which can be tolerated only if it is heavily regulated. Whilst the Conservatives have offered rhetorical support for private landlords, they have tended to be far more concerned with owner occupation. Housing policy debate and the use of financial supports have therefore been targeted to either social housing or owner occupation. As a result, private renting has been squeezed.

Attempts at reform

But this does not mean that there have been no attempts to reform the sector, merely that the sector has not been at the forefront of housing policy. As we have discussed, the Conservative government under Margaret Thatcher introduced the Housing Act 1988, seeing the abolition of rent control as a way of encouraging the sector. Whilst, as Wilcox (1999) has stated, this has led to a small increase in activity, it has not had a fundamental effect. This is largely because the private rented sector is now so small that it can have only a marginal impact. Several attempts, though, have been made to try to increase its size and therefore its significance, by encouraging either new development or the transfer of existing stock.

In 1988 the Business Expansion Scheme (BES, initially established in 1983) was extended to cover new equity investment in companies providing residential lettings. A private investor could receive tax relief at the marginal rate on up to £40,000 invested in shares of a BES company each year. It was a requirement that the investment be maintained for a minimum of five years, at which point holdings could be sold free of capital gains tax. No new schemes have been allowed since 1993 and thus all schemes were wound up by 1998. The scheme did have some effect on the sector, leading to the development of 81,000 new dwellings. Crook and Kemp (1996) show that in excess of £3 billion was raised by over 900 BES companies. They calculate that the net tax expenditure was £28,000 per dwelling, or 48 per cent of capital cost.

The key problem, however, was that the very nature of the business expansion scheme did not encourage a long-term commitment to the sector. BES companies were primarily used as vehicles for those seeking short-term capital gains. Nevertheless, the scheme did indicate that it was possible to encourage investment in the sector, if government was prepared to make the effort.

Perhaps a cheaper means of reinvigorating private renting, although without any net increase in the total housing stock, could be achieved through transferring social housing to private landlords. Local authority stock, as we have seen in Chapter 3, has been transferred consistently to new housing associations through the LSVT mechanism.

In the Finance Act 1996 the Conservative government established Housing Investment Trusts (HITs). This was a similar idea to the BES in that the scheme seeks to attract private investment to HITs, which would own private residential dwellings. Investors would benefit from reduced levels of corporation tax and exemption from capital gains tax. However, HITs differ from the BES in that they will purchase existing property rather than build new dwellings. They were therefore mainly intended as vehicles for the privatisation of local authority stock. It was significant that the Conservative government, if re-elected, had intended to insist that local authorities include transfer proposals in the HIP bids in 1997. As this transfer proposal was dropped when Labour was elected, it is perhaps not surprising that HITs have not developed as an investment vehicle for the private sector. That said, the Labour government announced in late 1999 an increase in the number of transfers it is prepared to allow. The 2000 housing green paper (DETR, 2000a) envisages a further increase in stock transfer with up to 200,000 being transferred per annum. But this proposal seems more likely to continue the trend towards diversity amongst social landlords, rather than encouraging private landlords themselves.

However, if this proposal is followed through, it will see the withering away of local authorities in around fifteen years. Depending on the vehicles used for stock transfer, this is bound to have a considerable impact on the private sector and lead to a vastly changed relationship between the tenures. It might lead towards the model in several European countries where the emphasis is less on ownership and more on who gains access to the stock (Oxley, 2000).

What future for private renting?

The 2000 housing green paper (DETR, 2000a) proposes no major transformation of the private rented sector. The Labour government seeks no drastic structural changes. It claims that it will respect the rights of landlords, but in return it wishes to ensure that landlords 'must do right by their tenants' (Armstrong, 1999b, p. 128). This implies an increase in regulation, particularly regarding the use of tenants' deposits by landlords and the licensing of houses in multiple occupation.

This intention is seen in the proposals in the green paper to offer local authorities the discretionary power to license problem properties or all private-sector stock in certain areas as a means of improving the quality of the stock. On a more positive note, the green paper discusses the possibility of RSLs acting as managing agents for small private landlords. It also proposes to investigate tax changes to make investment in the sector more attractive.

Whilst the green paper postpones any fundamental reform of housing benefit, it does propose further measures to deal with fraud (see Chapter 8 for a fuller discussion on housing benefit). These measures include closer liaison between local authorities and the DSS, and the establishment of a national fraud hotline. More specific to the private rented sector, the green paper proposes possible restrictions on payments to private landlords of substandard dwellings by either reducing payments or refusing to make direct payments to landlords. The government is conscious here of the need not to harm tenants' interests, and therefore the green paper appears to favour the banning of direct payments rather than reducing the level of payments. The latter appears to be an option only in areas of low demand, which would imply that tenants would have an alternative. This might have a considerable impact on the behaviour of private landlords, as the green paper suggests that 70 per cent of private tenants currently have their housing benefit paid direct to their landlord (DETR, 2000a). An extension of this proposal to cover all private tenants would have a considerable impact on fraud as well as fundamentally altering the relationship between landlord and tenant (King, 1999).

It is perhaps safe to say that private renting in the next decade is not likely to grow significantly, but nor will it shrink away. Indeed, the postponement of housing benefit offers some prospect of stability. Private renting might be a residual tenure, but there is still a sufficient demand from students, young people, transient households and those who cannot gain access to social housing.

ACTIVITY 6.4

What is the future role of the private rented sector?

Summary

In this chapter I have:

- considered the reasons for the decline of the private rented sector;

- discussed the particular forms of regulation in the sector, particularly rent controls;

- considered the various attempts to reform private renting and arrest its long-term decline;

- shown through the history of rent controls in the private sector that there are frequently unintended consequences of government action and that housing policy has long-term consequences; and

- shown that it is not possible to separate the fortunes of one tenure from another and that social housing and owner occupation in particular have benefited at the expense of private renting.

Further reading

For detailed coverage of the effects of rent control, see Albon and Stafford (1987). Hayek (1960) also has an interesting chapter on housing and planning which deals with the effects of intervening in rental markets. For discussion on the motivations of private landlords and the effects of government rent and housing benefit policy, see Bevan *et al.* (1995) and DETR (1999). A special issue of the journal *Housing Studies* (vol. 11, no. 1, 1996) deals with the private rented sector.

Owner occupation

- The political significance of owner occupation
- The scale of owner occupation as the dominant tenure
- How owner occupation is subsidised and how subsidies have changed over time
- What current policies are and the future prospects for the tenure

Introduction

There is an interesting divergence in the manner in which housing policy is discussed. Most academics and housing lobbyists tend to concentrate on social housing. The majority of writing on housing is about social housing, and most housing textbooks (including this one) are dominated by this sector. However, when politicians and the mass media concern themselves with housing it is more likely to be over owner occupation. Of course, many academics and commentators have waxed long and hard over policies such as the right to buy and the use of Housing Corporation funds to boost the housing market. But most of these criticisms are based on the impact that these policies have had on the social rented sector. It is the loss of 1.3 million council dwellings and the resultant residualisation of the sector which vexes critics, not the increased choice offered to households exercising their right to buy.

But while academics talk and write, it is the politicians who can actually change things. Academics, lobbyists and social housing professionals might rant and rail, but the priorities are set by politicians and their perceptions of what is necessary (and, they hope, popular). As a result, the emphasis in housing policy-making since the mid-1970s has shifted in favour of owner occupation. This is part of the more general shift towards market solutions which put greater emphasis on choice and individual responsibility that we noted in Chapter 2 (and will discuss again in Chapter 9).

ACTIVITY 7.1

Discuss why owner occupation is so popular in the UK.

In this chapter I want to explore why owner occupation has become so significant relative to the other housing tenures. I shall begin this chapter by exploring the politics of owner occupation. I shall then examine the effects that owner occupation has had, and hence why it is important politically. This will lead on to a discussion of the subsidies that have been offered to the tenure and the effects that they have had. Finally, I shall examine current government policy towards owner occupation.

The politics of owner occupation

Owner occupation is the dominant tenure in Britain, with 69 per cent of households in this sector (Table 7.1). In that sense it could be said to be the 'normal' tenure, in that a majority of households either enjoy it already or aspire to it. When housing is discussed by politicians, and when it becomes important politically, it is usually owner occupation and the need for building new private housing that are the focus of attention. Thus over the past twenty years the issues of rising and falling house prices, repossessions and building on the green belt have proved to be much more sensitive issues than homelessness and the state of repair of the local authority stock. It is noteworthy that, insofar as housing is ever discussed in the annual Budget, the concentration is on mortgages and the sustainability of the owner-occupied sector.

Table 7.1 *Growth of owner occupation in the UK*

Year	Percentage of households
1914	10
1945	26
1951	29
1961	43
1971	53
1981	56
1991	66
2000	69

Sources: DETR (2000a); Malpass and Murie (1999); Wilcox (2000)

This situation, however, is not particularly surprising, for two reasons. First, one should not be taken aback that governments concentrate on what is popular for the majority. There are twice as many households in the owner-occupied sector as in the private and social rented sectors combined. Owner occupiers are more likely to vote and thus cannot be taken for granted by politicians. There is a perception that council tenants either won't vote or will vote Labour. Either way they can be taken for granted! The crude fact is that for politicians, owning matters more than renting.

Second, because of this popularity, owner occupation has been the focus of government housing policy since 1979 and thus at the forefront of thinking and action on housing. The Conservatives maintained financial supports to owner occupation, even though they sought to deregulate in other areas. Indeed, they presented the tenure as desirable in itself. This was shown by their two main ideological statements on housing. The white papers of both 1987 and 1995 express explicit support for this tenure (DoE, 1987, 1995). The 1987 white paper suggested that tax relief was justified whereas subsidies to housing associations were too generous. The 1995 white paper proposed that the majority of housing need over the next fifteen years should be met by owner occupation with a view to increasing the proportion to 80 per cent of households.

Of course, these two issues are linked. Politicians do things they think will be popular (even if they claim to be taking 'hard' decisions), but then things do tend to increase in popularity if they are subsidised by government. Unravelling this situation – is owner occupation popular because it has been subsidised or has it been subsidised because it is popular? – is virtually impossible. However, as we shall see later in the chapter, government supports to owner occupation have reduced since the early 1990s without any great reduction in perceived popularity of the tenure (although this reduction in support did coincide with a considerable drop in the popularity of the Major government).

It is important to appreciate right at the start of our discussion on owner occupation that the tenure is not independent of the rented sectors. The Conservatives used social housing provision in order to enhance owner occupation. The most obvious example of this is the right-to-buy policy introduced in the Housing Act 1980. Therefore owner occupation had grown directly at the expense of local authority housing, with 1.3 million tenants exercising their right to buy (DETR, 2000a).

This use of the social sector can also be seen in the shift in priorities of the Housing Corporation's Approved Development Programme towards ownership initiatives, such as low-cost home ownership and the Tenants' Incentive Scheme. Money which hitherto would have been used to build or renovate social housing was increasingly being used to further encourage owner occupation.

The popular conception of the politics of owner occupation which used to hold can be summed up by a rather old (and bad) joke:

HUSBAND: Well, that's the mortgage paid off.
WIFE: Thank goodness for that, now we can vote Labour again!

The belief was that increasing owner occupation would encourage people to vote Conservative. This was because only the Conservatives could be trusted to support owner occupiers, whilst the Labour Party was stuck to its policy of supporting social housing. The Thatcher government appeared to believe there was a positive link between voting Conservative and owner occupation when it proclaimed the aim of creating a 'property-owning democracy'. Whilst this phrase had been used by Conservative politicians since Anthony Eden in the 1950s, it became a central plank of government social policy in the 1980s. On the one hand, the Conservatives encouraged greater share ownership, particularly in the privatised utilities. On the other, they encouraged the spread of owner occupation, particularly through the right to buy, but also through deregulation of the mortgage market and through a generally supportive rhetoric.

There has been considerable academic debate about whether there is a link between voting and tenure (Saunders, 1990). The Conservatives themselves, on the basis of the vigour with which they supported owner occupation, clearly believed that there was such a link. They believed that increasing owner occupation would increase social stability and give households a greater stake in the nation's prosperity. These were seen as conservative values and would thus have a positive electoral impact.

But attempting to prove whether there is a link between voting and tenure is beyond the remit of this book. Indeed, in some ways the question has lost much of its relevance. This is because there is now a political consensus about the central place of owner occupation as the tenure of choice (DETR, 2000a).

The Labour Party opposed the right to buy on its introduction, and indeed its 1983 election manifesto committed the party to repealing the legislation. The huge defeat of Labour in that election led its strategists to rethink their policies on housing (as with much else), and by 1987 they had accepted the right to buy as a popular policy. The Labour government elected in 1997 has modified the right to buy by limiting the discounts available, but has not altered eligibility. Indeed, the 2000 green paper admits that the policy has been successful in helping '1.3 million council tenants to realise their aspirations to own their own homes' (DETR, 2000a, p. 36). As a result, the Labour government intends to maintain the right to buy into the future.

But the Labour government's support for owner occupation goes further. The 2000 green paper is clear in its support for the tenure: 'Homeownership is the most popular choice of housing in England. Over 14 million households (69 per cent) are owner-occupiers and, in surveys, up to 90 per cent of people say that homeownership is their preferred choice' (DETR, 2000a, p. 30).

So both main parties have coalesced around a policy of supporting owner occupation. However, as we shall see later in the chapter, the nature of this support has changed. Instead of there being direct subsidies to owner occupiers the emphasis is now on creating the right economic conditions to sustain owner occupation.

The scale of owner occupation

To grasp its political significance, we need to appreciate the scale of owner occupation in the UK. This will allow us to understand why it might have such an impact on the economy and the political system.

The key facts about owner occupation are as follows:

- Sixty-nine per cent of households are owner occupiers.
- This equates to 16.7 million dwellings in the UK out of a total of 24.8 million.
- Wilcox (1999) calculated the total value of the owner-occupied stock in the UK in 1998 at £1,265 billion, which is equivalent to 151 per cent of the gross domestic product.
- He calculates house purchase debt at £452 billion, which means that there is £812 billion of free equity which households might be able to use to purchase other goods and services.
- In 1998, mortgage lenders made 1.03 million mortgage advances totalling £24 billion.
- Average house prices for the UK have increased from £23,596 in 1980 to £81,994 in 1998.
- But there are considerable regional variations in house prices, with the average for the north of England in 1999 being £63,500 whilst the average for Greater London was £142,694.
- In 1999 average male earnings were £23,005 (£442.40 per week) and

female earnings were £16,978 (£326.50 per week), which would fund a maximum mortgage for a working couple of just over £70,000.

- Interest rates have varied considerably over the past thirty years, with a high of 15 per cent in 1990 and a low of 6.7 per cent in 1996.
- However, interest rates have been below 8 per cent since 1993.
- The average monthly repayment for a first-time buyer was £20.83 in 1970, £122.60 in 1980 and £375.47 in 1998.
- Since 1970, average house prices have fallen only in one year (by 0.2 per cent in 1992).
- The highest annual increase was 23.1 per cent in 1988.

What these figures show is that funding owner occupation will take up a significant portion of the average household budget, although it is cheaper in the later 1990s and early 2000s than for the previous three decades, and that housing markets involve huge sums of money. It is therefore hardly surprising that the owner-occupied market matters so much to both government and individual households.

As we have seen, the Conservative governments between 1979 and 1997 realised that owner occupation met the aspirations of the majority of households. Somewhat belatedly, the Labour Party came to accept this as legitimate. It was therefore quite rational for elected politicians to support owner occupation. But the importance of owner occupation goes beyond electoral considerations to include a number of political and economic questions. Indeed, the significance of owner occupation is not merely its popularity, but the effect that it has in economic and political terms. We need to appreciate these wider effects if we are to fully understand the owner-occupied sector and the manner in which it has been supported.

The importance of owner occupation as a consumption good

Housing costs are usually the largest single item in any household's budget. The large portion of household income taken up with housing means that changes in housing costs are likely to have considerable effects on total household consumption. A general increase in housing costs, through an increase in the cost of borrowing, has major economic effects, as was shown in the early 1990s when interest rates rose to 15 per cent. These effects go beyond housing and affect demand in other markets, as households have less disposable income after housing costs.

But it is this very effect which makes housing costs particularly susceptible to government intervention to meet its wider macroeconomic policy aims. With the trend against the use of fiscal policies of increasing taxation or increasing government spending to control the economy, interest rates have become an increasingly important means of controlling the economy. Government, therefore, in effect targets the housing costs of owner occupiers as a way of controlling the economy.

This was particularly the case in the early 1990s when the Major government tried to reduce inflation from the 9.5 per cent it reached in 1990. The result was an increase in mortgage repossessions from 15,810 in 1989 to 75,540 in 1991 and an increase in the number of those with more than six months' mortgage arrears from 80,640 in 1989 to 275,350 two years later. In addition, many households saw the value of their dwellings fall, leaving 1.77 million owner occupiers in 1992 with negative equity, meaning that their outstanding debt was greater than the value of the property (Wilcox, 1997).

On one level the policy was successful in that it did rein in consumer spending and reduce inflation to historically low levels. One could also state that the prolonged slump in the housing market has led to a shift in attitudes about owner occupation, which makes future property booms less likely (although this is by no means proven). However, if one delves below the macroeconomic level one sees a considerable amount of broken aspirations, anxiety and despair as families either lost their homes or saw property values plummet.

One of the problems of this policy is that it is a rather blunt instrument. Government might be able to alter the direction in which the economy is moving. But this does not mean that it can control the exact extent of the movement and ensure that any changes are limited to what is strictly necessary.

The boom and slump in housing between 1985 and 1993 showed the political significance of owner occupation. The boom created a 'feel-good factor' which the government could claim the credit for. In the 1980s the Conservatives clearly benefited from being the party of owner occupation. However, this close association came to be seen as a liability when house prices slumped and repossessions and negative equity increased.

One can only speculate on the connection between the Major government's unpopularity after 1992 and the housing slump. Whilst issues such as the humiliating withdrawal from the Exchange Rate

Mechanism in September 1992 might have had more impact on the government's standing, its inability to reverse the slump in the housing market did not help the government to recover. The impact of the slump in the early 1990s was therefore much greater than the Major government would have wished.

A further economic effect of owner occupation is the so-called *cascade effect* whereby housing wealth is passed on from one generation to the next. Most children will inherit the property of their parents, and this effectively liquidates the wealth stored in the property. This means that the wealth of a significant number of households, most of whom are already owner occupiers, is further enhanced. As a result, the wealth generated by owner occupation tends to become polarised, with some households quite asset rich, owing to inheritance, whilst renters (who also are often following a generational pattern) miss out.

Derived demand

Owner occupation is economically important because there is a lot of derived demand resulting from owner occupation. This is market activity which arises as a result of transactions in the housing market. Many markets depend upon an active housing market. For example, the demand for DIY products, home furnishing, white goods and insurance in each case depends on a vibrant housing market. In addition, many solicitors depend on their conveyancing business, and estate agents are particularly susceptible to changes in the market as they rely entirely on the level of sales. A boom or slump in the housing market has considerable spillover effects and thus owner occupation should not be taken in isolation.

We should also remember that housebuilding is labour intensive and not particularly import sensitive. Thus an active housing market, which encourages new development, can have an effect on unemployment.

Interestingly, however, the slump in the housing market did help to halt the decline in the private rented sector. Many households, either because of negative equity or the state of the market, were unable or unwilling to sell their property, even when they had purchased another. They were able to recoup their costs by letting the property until market conditions improved. The introduction of assured shorthold tenancies in 1989 made letting more attractive, as did the opportunity to charge rents at market levels. Sadly, one could also suggest that the increase in the number of households who suffered from repossession merely bolstered the demand for private rented housing.

The divergence of cost and value

This issue of negative equity highlights a further facet of owner-occupied housing. Owing to the way in which housing is financed, there may often be a significant divergence between a household's regular costs (i.e. mortgage repayments) and the value of the dwelling. This can create a considerable benefit to households in that the value of their dwelling has increased whilst their mortgage costs have remained static. They are thus able to tap into the free equity of their property to fund additional expenditure. However, in the early 1990s there were many households for whom the value of their property was less than their mortgage. This might mean they could not afford to sell the dwelling. The problem is often compounded by the fact that as housing costs rise, house values decline because owner occupation becomes less attractive.

It is the nature of the financing of owner occupation which creates this situation. Properties are usually purchased using long-term mortgage finance. The amount borrowed obviously relates to the value of the dwelling, although the actual percentage will differ depending on the lender's policy and practice, the household's usable savings and whether the households are first-time buyers or existing owners moving on.

However, over time the positive relationship between cost and value will weaken. There may be a correlation between housing costs and house prices at the national level, in that lower housing costs will encourage demand and this may cause prices to rise. However, for any individual household the relationship will tend to diverge. This is because housing costs and house values are not necessarily determined by the same factors. Mortgage costs may rise as interest rates go up, as occurred in the early 1990s. They might also rise because of changes in government policy, such as the phasing out of mortgage interest tax relief. But this may not have a direct effect on the value of one's dwelling. One may own a property in a sought-after area, causing it to increase in value more rapidly than a similar property in another area. Until the 1990s, house prices tended to rise faster than earnings or inflation. Therefore over time one would expect the value of one's property to increase in real terms.

Indeed, one of the most important issues is when the property was purchased. It is perfectly possible for one household to be paying twice as much as their neighbour for a similar property. This is simply because of when they bought it. If one took out a mortgage of £23,600 to purchase the average house in 1980, then one is still paying a mortgage based on that cost even though the value of that average house is now over £80,000. But anyone purchasing the average dwelling today must expect to repay a mortgage based on a property valuation of £80,000 plus. Moreover, if they took out a mortgage when interest rates were high, they would obviously have to pay more. Therefore the actual housing costs of households will differ quite markedly, and the type and location of property will offer only a rough guide to housing costs.

The traditional 'common-sense' advice given to first-time buyers was to borrow as much as they could afford, on the premise that incomes and house values tend to rise in real terms, but housing costs stay static. Thus housing costs might take up 40 per cent of the household budget in year one, but by year ten this might have reduced to only 15 per cent. This model of relatively stable house price inflation and incomes growth tended to hold through much of the last half of the twentieth century and led to considerable increases in household wealth. However, it does make first-time buyers susceptible to the impoverishing effects of rapid increases in housing costs, as occurred in the early 1990s. Consequently, it does tend to be the most recent first-time buyers who have borne the brunt of housing slumps. We shall return to this issue towards the end of this chapter when we consider current government policies.

The divergence between the cost and value of housing over time is also important in another sense. Households have been able to use the increased value of their property to fund additional expenditure, such as starting a business, paying school fees, buying new cars, boats, holidays, as well as funding improvements to the property itself. This is commonly known as *equity withdrawal*.

The unknown cost of housing

The fact that housing costs change over time raises another important point about owner occupation. Not only is a property the most expensive item one is ever likely to buy, it is also the only commodity one will purchase without knowledge of its final costs.

Of course, most households will take out loans or hire purchase agreements to fund certain goods or services, such as a car or a personal computer. However, these are usually at fixed rates of interest and over a short period of time. Thus we know exactly how much we will have to repay and can budget accordingly.

But because interest rates are likely to change over the twenty-five years of the average mortgage repayment period, we do not know what we will actually pay until the mortgage has finally been paid off. Increasingly, mortgage lenders are introducing a degree of stability into the market by offering fixed-rate mortgages, but these are seldom for more than five or ten years. Indeed, with the great variation in interest rates over the past thirty years it would not necessarily be very sensible to be locked into a fixed rate for too long a period (unless, of course, it was especially low).

However, even if one did take out a twenty-five-year fixed-rate mortgage, one could still not be certain of the total cost to the household. This is because government policies might change in ways that are unforeseen. In 1987 the Liberal Democrats launched themselves as a new party with a commitment (amongst other things) to the withdrawal of mortgage interest tax relief (MITR). Within twenty-four hours this policy was rescinded on the grounds it was electorally suicidal for any party to seriously propose it. The Liberal Democrats reverted to the same policy of Labour and the Conservatives of retaining MITR. Yet the political climate had changed to such an extent that MITR had been entirely phased out by 2000. The key issue here is that no one could rationally expect national housing policy to remain unchanged for twenty-five years, a period that would span at least five general elections.

Therefore, whilst long-term finance makes owner occupation affordable to the majority, it also carries with it a number of uncertainties as to the final cost that any household will incur. Owner occupation may be a relatively safe gamble, but it is a gamble nonetheless.

A perverse form of support

A further distinctive factor about owner occupation has been the manner in which it is treated by government. Unlike subsidies to social housing and private tenants, the main financial support to owner occupation, MITR, was not provided on the basis of need, but rather was *universal*, in that all households paying tax with a mortgage were

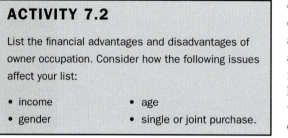

ACTIVITY 7.2

List the financial advantages and disadvantages of owner occupation. Consider how the following issues affect your list:

- income
- gender
- age
- single or joint purchase.

entitled to it. Other tax exemptions which still apply are equally universal in their application. Subsidy is indiscriminate and unrelated to household income in a way which does not apply to any other housing sector. But as we shall see in the next section, this is by no means the only difference between the support given to owning and renting.

Subsidy

The Conservative governments of Margaret Thatcher and John Major portrayed the virtues of owner occupation in terms of the fostering of the values of independence and personal responsibility. Likewise the Blair government supports the tenure because it allows people to fulfil their aspirations. However, this does not mean that governments have just allowed individuals to get on with it. In fact the reverse is the case.

Since the Second World War, owner occupation has been actively supported by rhetoric, but also by means of subsidy. Indeed, as we have seen, the Conservative government, in its 1987 white paper (DoE, 1987), argued that the continuance of subsidies to owner occupation was fully justified, whilst questioning the level of subsidy to social housing. But this subsidy to owner occupation was justified precisely because of the supposed values which the tenure encouraged, namely, self-reliance and responsibility.

Whilst the financial support given has decreased in recent years, as the availability of improvement grants has reduced and MITR has been abolished, the tenure is still subsidised through a number of tax exemptions which give it favourable treatment in relation to private-sector landlords in particular.

What is important about subsidies to owner occupation, though, is that they have been unrelated to access and affordability. Existing tax reliefs are universal, and MITR applied to all households with a mortgage who paid tax. This form of subsidy was increasingly anomalous, in that there has been a general trend towards targeted means-tested benefits as the primary means of delivering welfare support. The effect of MITR in particular was in fact regressive in that until 1991 it was possible to get tax relief at the highest rate of tax one paid. This actively benefited the better-off. One can therefore legitimately argue that MITR was a blatantly political form of support in order to favour a popular activity. Of course, once it had become sufficiently well established, and seen as a normal part of the housing market – remember, it was taken off mortgage payments and thus no money went through purse or wallet – it was felt to be politically difficult if not impossible to abolish it.

But subsidies offered to owner occupation differ from those to social housing in a further way. Unlike housing benefit, HRA subsidy or social housing grant, owner occupation is subsidised through *tax expenditures*. These can be defined *as the failure to levy a tax* – where government offers tax relief on a certain activity, rather than offering a direct subsidy. It is called expenditure because it reduces government revenues in the same way as spending would. But there is no direct transfer from government to beneficiary, rather a reduction in the amount of tax taken by government.

Some have argued that tax relief is not a subsidy at all because government does not make any payments and government itself, as a practice, does not directly include tax relief as housing expenditure. Indeed, it was not until the 1995 white paper (DoE, 1995) that any government admitted that MITR was indeed a subsidy. Previously, government ministers had argued that all they were doing was allowing households to keep more of their own money.

The issue properly depends upon whether it would be normal for owner occupiers to pay tax on all their income or whether it is normal that they receive a rebate on that part of their income used to pay their mortgage. However, the tax relief exists only because of a special provision and therefore it is a subsidy, even if it is an implicit rather than explicit one.

Mortgage interest tax relief (MITR)

MITR was finally phased out completely in April 2000. However, it had been of such importance to the development of owner occupation, and a source of such controversy, that we still need to consider it.

MITR, or, as it was sometimes referred to, MIRAS (mortgage interest relief at source, in that it was deducted at source rather than having to be individually claimed), was allowed on the interest payments of the first £30,000 of a mortgage loan. This £30,000 figure had not been uprated since 1981 and thus its real effect had declined considerably as house prices rose to an average of over £80,000 by the end of the 1990s.

MITR had increased considerably throughout the 1980s. In 1979/80, 5.9 million recipients received a total of £1,450 million, making an average relief of £250 per recipient per year. However, in 1990/1, 9.6 million recipients received a total of £7,700 million at an average of £820 per person per year. Subsequently MITR declined to £1.5 million in 1999/2000, although the number of recipients increased to over 10 million. It was abolished entirely in 2000.

The decline in MITR had come about for a number of reasons. The most important was that interest rates in the 1990s were considerably lower than in the 1980s. One received relief as a fixed percentage of the amount of interest one paid and this proved to be a declining amount over the 1990s. A subsidiary point is that, as most recipients received relief at the basic rate of income tax, cuts in taxation from 31 per cent in 1990 to 23 per cent in 1999/2000 also reduced the amount one received.

But there had also been consistent attempts since the late 1980s to reduce tax relief. It was common knowledge that the Chancellor of the Exchequer between 1983 and 1989, Nigel Lawson, wanted to abolish MITR on the grounds that it distorted the proper operation of the housing market. As a demand-led subsidy it was difficult to control, because government could not restrict the number of eligible recipients. However, he was overruled by Margaret Thatcher, the Prime Minister, who saw the political advantages of its maintenance. But Lawson and his successors were able to reduce its impact:

- The limit for the receipt of relief was not increased from £30,000, despite significant house price inflation in the 1980s.
- Up to 1989, relief was available to all those party to the mortgage. After 1989 only one amount of relief was permitted per dwelling.
- Prior to 1991, tax relief could be claimed at the marginal highest rate of tax one paid. MITR was limited to the basic rate from 1991.
- Subsequently MITR was reduced to 20 per cent in 1994/5 and 15 per cent in 1995/6. It was reduced again in April 1998 down to 10 per cent. It was phased out entirely in April 2000.

This latter point is interesting in that, as stated several times above, politicians had felt that MITR was untouchable. However, a policy of steady cutbacks, coupled with low inflation and low interest rates, had taken the sting out of this issue and allowed it to be finally done away with, apparently without any great political controversy. This shows that significant changes can occur, but that quite often they occur slowly and are at the mercy of events beyond the direct control of politicians.

Other tax exemptions

Despite the abolition of MITR, a number of other forms of tax relief remain. First – and this is a benefit shared with rented housing – owner occupation is exempted from VAT. The reason for this was that the consumption of housing is already taxed through the council tax, which is partially related to property values.

Second, unlike private landlords, owner occupiers do not pay tax on the capital gains made on the sale of an asset. This would normally be at the marginal income tax rate. The main reason for exemption is that an owner frequently uses the receipts of the sale to fund another purchase. It has also been argued that to impose this tax would be to reduce mobility and depress the market. However, others have argued that to impose it would reduce under-occupation and volatility in the housing market by reducing speculative purchases.

Third, since 1962, owner occupiers have been exempt from *imputed rental income tax* or *Schedule A* taxation. This now appears a rather odd idea, but prior to 1962 it was assumed that an owner, because he or she did not have to pay rent for their dwelling, was in receipt of a potential benefit over that enjoyed by tenants. Owners were able to spend that income they would otherwise have to spend on rent. Thus, it was argued, owning rather than renting led to an increase in disposable income. Owner occupiers were therefore taxed at the marginal rate on the imputed rent for that property (i.e. what rent could be charged).

Against Schedule A taxation, however, owner occupiers could deduct legitimate expenses, particularly interest payments. This is what developed into MITR. However, when Schedule A taxation for owner occupiers was abolished in 1962, tax relief on mortgage interest was retained, even though the original justification for it no longer applied.

Financial deregulation

Whilst subsidies have been important in the growth and sustainability of owner occupation, the tenure was also given a considerable impetus by the deregulation of the financial markets in the 1980s. The Building Societies Act 1986 scrapped many of the restrictions on building society lending and allowed societies to diversify. Regulations were also changed, allowing banks to compete in the mortgage market. In 1983, 79 per cent of mortgages were obtained through a building society, and only 15 per cent from banks. By 1998 the figures were 22 per cent for building societies and 65 per cent for banks. This was partly because of the number of large building societies such as Abbey and Halifax that have demutualised and become banks. But it has also been due to a significant increase in competition, in which lenders became rather more flexible in their lending policies. In particular, mortgage lenders in the late 1980s allowed applicants to borrow more.

ACTIVITY 7.3

Explain the key differences between subsidies to owner occupation and those to rented housing. What accounts for the differential treatment?

But this policy, whilst allowing greater access to owner occupation, led to the instability of the later 1980s and early 1990s, which saw the virtual doubling of house prices in the south of England, followed by an almost equivalent fall in values. It was this volatility, and the consequent unpopularity of the Conservative government, that led to a change in policy.

Changing policies

The Major government's first reaction to the housing slump in the early 1990s was to try to encourage market activity through measures targeted at households under threat of repossession. In 1991 it introduced a mortgage-to-rent scheme aimed at encouraging mortgage lenders to loan funds to housing associations so that the latter could buy up properties before they were repossessed. The owner occupier would then revert to being a sitting tenant. The mortgage lender would thus be transferring a loan from the mortgagee to the housing association. However, these proposals did not lead anywhere, largely because of the reluctance of all parties and because government offered no financial encouragement.

A further attempt was therefore made in 1992/3 in the so-called Housing Market Package (HMP), which brought forward £579 million of Housing Corporation funding to be used to purchase (at prevailing grant rates) properties on the open market. The idea was that this would kick-start the moribund housing market. However, a scheme that bought up only 18,000 dwellings was unlikely to have a major impact. Indeed, the major long-term impact was on housing associations, which saw the Housing Corporation's Approved Development Programme cut back drastically in the years following.

The policy of the Major government towards owner occupation changed considerably after the failure of the HMP to have any great impact. The new Chancellor of the Exchequer in 1993, Kenneth Clarke, took the view that the HMP was a waste of money which had merely benefited private developers. Moreover, there was now ample evidence that government policy might actually have the effect of destabilising housing markets. This was partly because of the effects of subsidies, which serve to encourage demand and lead to periodic shortages in supply.

But the main reason for the change in policy was a broadening understanding of the embedded nature of owner occupation in the wider economy. Government now appeared to grasp that what mattered most was not tax relief, but secure employment prospects, stable interest rates and low inflation. What the housing market needed from government was economic stability so that house prices did not rise too quickly and so that mortgage rates were stable and affordable. Hence the Major government began the process of phasing out MITR in 1994/5.

This policy has been maintained by the Labour government since 1997. It continued to phase out MITR, and abolished it completely in 2000. Moreover, it appears to concur with Clarke's view on the need for stability. The 2000 green paper states:

> The main contribution government can make to sustainable homeownership is a robust economy in all parts of the country and a strong system of consumer protection. As a result of our economic policies, homeowners are benefiting from relatively low mortgage interest rates and rising living standards. ... We are determined to avoid a return to the boom and bust economy of the past, which eroded the security many expected from their homes and created an uncertain climate for one of the most important long-term financial commitments which most people make.
>
> (DETR, 2000a, p. 30)

In consequence, Labour's proposals to develop owner occupation in the 2000 green paper are quite modest. Many commentators picked up the so-called Starter Home Initiative (SHI), which offers financial support to key workers, such as nurses and teachers, in high-cost areas. However, the extent and scope of this proposal are still unclear. Other measures in the green paper deal with reducing eligibility to income support payments to cover mortgage payments and a review of local authorities' role in maintaining and improving the standard of the stock in their locality. There is, though, no promise of additional funding attached to this potential change.

One can state therefore that there has been a consensus over policy towards owner occupation since 1993. Economic stability is now seen as the best way of sustaining owner occupation, and it is accepted that large-scale government intervention is both wasteful and ineffective. There is now a recognition that it is not government policy directly which affects the housing market, but external factors, such as job security, unemployment and interest rates. Accordingly, it is better for government to concentrate on general economic policy and leave households to actually make the self-reliant choices both the Conservatives and Labour believe they aspire to. As a result, much of the politics has been taken out of housing.

Summary

In this chapter I have:

- considered why owner occupation is of such political significance compared to social and private renting;
- discussed the scale of the tenure in economic and monetary terms;
- looked at the particular nature of owner occupation in relation to household budgets, derived demand, the divergence of cost and value;
- explained the distinctive nature of subsidies to owner occupation, based on universal principles rather than need;
- considered the reasons for the withdrawal of mortgage interest tax relief; and
- suggested that policy supporting owner occupation is now based on economic stability rather than direct government intervention.

Further reading

The most useful source of information on owner occupation is the annual *Housing Finance Review* (Wilcox, 2000 is the latest edition), which contains myriad facts and figures on the sector. Other interesting information is given in the quarterly journal *Housing Finance*, published by the Council for Mortgage Lenders.

The best overall discussion on owner occupation (and not just financial issues) is that by Saunders (1990). The book is written from a committed Conservative position and is quite complex in places, but it summarises the literature on the tenure. An influential Marxist discussion is offered by Ball (1983). Another useful, and more introductory, text is that by Forrest *et al.* (1990). For a discussion that puts British owner occupation into a European context, see McCrone and Stephens (1995). A good discussion of the historical development of owner occupation as a tenure is given by Daunton (1987).

8 Housing benefit

- The nature of the current housing benefit system
- The key problem areas in the operation of the system including the differences between tenures
- Why reform of housing benefit is so difficult
- Proposals for reforming housing benefit

Introduction

Housing benefit is the problem that won't go away, but no one, least of all government, can decide how to deal with. Throughout 1999, government ministers indicated that major reforms to housing benefit were to be proposed in the housing green paper due out in that year. However, as the leaves fell from the trees, the promised green paper failed to appear and ministers became much more guarded about reforming housing benefit. When the green paper was finally published in April 2000 the issue of housing benefit reform had been superseded by other priorities. Minor changes were proposed, but the overhauling of the benefit system was to be put off for a decade.

However, the green paper (DETR, 2000a) is still fulsome in its condemnation of the housing benefit system. The relevant chapter contains a long list of the system's faults. What it doesn't do is offer any positive proposals for dealing with these faults. This is a very strange situation: government identifies a major problem, but then says it is going to ignore it whilst it does other things. The government can see the problem, but either cannot or will not tackle it. The green paper ought to have been the culmination of a long and detailed debate about housing benefit and its future (Kemp, 1997, 1998, 2000; Wilcox, 1997). The green paper appeared to concur with many of the criticisms about housing benefit, in terms of complex administration, fraud, lack of incentives and so on. Yet it drew back from acting.

This is particularly odd in the light of one of the main themes of this book, namely, the centralisation of control. Governments, since the early 1970s, have centralised housing systems and certainly have not been afraid to act. Yet the actual prospect of housing benefit reform causes politicians to draw back and postpone any major changes. Why is this? Is there something particular about housing benefit that makes it impossible to change, even though everybody knows it is a mess?

In this chapter I wish to explore why this situation has come about and how it might be resolved. I shall look briefly at the key elements of the current benefit system and indicate how it operates with regard to the various different tenures. I shall then look at why housing benefit is considered to be a problem ripe for reform and, finally, what any possible reforms may look like. But first I shall further explore why reform is being stalled.

As in the other chapters in this book, I shall concentrate on the political issues surrounding the benefit system rather than covering the technical details of housing benefit. An understanding of what housing benefit is there to do and whether it does it effectively is one of the key issues with regard to housing finance at present. The ability to work out a claim for benefit is important, but it tells us little about the system itself. Moreover, the housing benefit system is so complex and ever-changing that any detailed coverage of how the system works would be out of date before this book were published.

Too big a problem to tackle?

In March 1999 the government announced that it would be publishing a green paper on housing policy. One of the three main areas it was intended to look at was the reform of housing benefit. The housing benefit system was seen as having weaknesses in that, to quote the then housing minister, it 'gives tenants little interest in their rent. It can also act as a disincentive to work. It is also extremely complex, making it difficult for claimants to understand, difficult for local authorities to administer, and prone to fraud' (Armstrong, 1999a, p. 14). Indeed, when the green paper finally appeared in April 2000, the problems of the current housing benefit system were clearly outlined. However, the only reform proposals the green paper discusses are a number of minor changes in administration and in the means of tackling fraud.

The government-stated case for inaction was that it needed to restructure rents and introduce choice into allocations: 'There would be little point in making these types of fundamental policy changes to Housing Benefit before rent restructuring' (DETR, 2000a, p. 115). But no further reason is given as to why this is the case. Indeed, if housing benefit does have an incentive effect on rents and the behaviour of landlords and tenants, one would have thought that reforming the benefit system might have been an effective way of restructuring rents. However, this choice of priorities effectively puts off the reform of housing benefit for up to ten years.

The real reason for delaying reform may have been that the government wished to duck the issue as being too difficult. Housing benefit is a major problem, but it is an intractable one with no obvious solution. In political terms, it is one in which the government would find little to benefit from. Any change to housing benefit entitlements would have been unpopular and have appeared draconian. As with all welfare reform, it is not possible to introduce change without at least some people being worse off as a result. As a result, politicians might prefer the existing seriously flawed system on the grounds that any other proposed system has flaws as well.

One fears that the problem might be that the government is not really clear what it is that it wishes to achieve from welfare reform. Is it intending to save money or is it trying to change behaviour and thereby reduce dependency on welfare? It may well be possible to achieve both at the same time, but this is unlikely. It is more likely that attempts to change behaviour will prove initially quite expensive, but with the promise of savings in the future. However, it was the refusal by the Treasury to countenance extra expenditure in the short term that apparently led Frank Field, the minister for welfare reform, to resign in July 1998 after just fifteen months in office.

But a refusal to tackle a problem does not mean it will go away. Since 1989, housing benefit has become increasingly important in housing policy. As we saw in Chapters 2 and 3, the Conservative government pursued a policy of shifting financial supports away from housing providers and towards individual households. The belief was that there was now enough housing to go round and therefore the emphasis should be on ensuring that households gain access to housing that is both of good quality and affordable. Housing policy should also seek to encourage choice and personal responsibility. As a result, housing benefit has had to 'take the strain' as rents have increased to compensate for reductions in public subsidies to local authorities and housing associations.

This shift towards personal subsidies is not confined to Britain; it is a phenomenon common to Europe, America and Australasia. Kemp (1997) suggests that this has been a general trend as what constituted the housing problem changed. The 1970s saw the end of massive housing shortages and thus the need for mass housebuilding programmes. This coincided with the world-wide economic slump of the 1970s, which led many politicians and commentators to question whether the welfare state was affordable in its current form. Targeted personal subsidies were now seen as cheaper and a more effective means of helping the poor. The 1970s and 1980s also saw a political sea change which favoured market solutions to social problems and gave a greater emphasis to the consumer over the producer. Some countries, such as Australia, New Zealand and the USA, have almost totally got rid of capital subsidies. However, Britain has not gone as far as this and still maintains a hybrid system of capital and personal subsidies. What this means, of course, is that the two forms of subsidy interact. In particular, it has been the withdrawal of capital subsidies, such as social housing grant, that has led to an increase in housing benefit.

It would not be going too far to suggest that the current systems of housing provision *depend upon* housing benefit. Private landlords would find it difficult to survive without it, with nearly 40 per cent of their tenants claiming benefit (see Table 8.1). But this dependency is even greater on the part of social landlords, with two-thirds of both local authority and housing association tenants in receipt of benefit. This means that in 1998, 57 per cent of tenants (private and social combined) were in receipt of housing benefit and therefore presumably would not be able to pay their rents without it. It is the housing benefit system which makes housing affordable to a majority of tenants and therefore it provides an income for landlords. As we shall see, it is not just tenants who are

Table 8.1 *Percentage of households in receipt of benefit by tenure, 1998*

Tenure	Number of households	Number of housing benefit recipients	Percentage
Local authority	4,117,000	2,664,000	65
Housing association	1,210,000	840,000	69
Private renting	2,581,000	970,000	38
Total	7,908,000	4,474,000	57

Source: Wilcox (2000)

dependent on housing benefit, but also private and social landlords. Reforming housing benefit would be to reform what is now the main source of income for landlords, particularly in the social rented sector. Any reform could therefore have a major destabilising effect on landlords, regardless of any impact it would have on tenants.

Therefore what makes the reform of housing benefit so difficult, even when the government sees that it is necessary, is this problem of dependency and just what would happen if it were reformed. Housing benefit, one fears, just might be too difficult to reform.

But is this really the case? Is housing benefit too difficult to reform, or is it just vested interests defending a system that works to their benefit? In the rest of this chapter I wish to explore these issues, by explaining the background to the debate and looking at certain features of the housing benefit system and some of the main proposals for its reform. In doing so I will show that the government does indeed face a major problem and that it is an extremely complex one. However, there is no evidence to suggest that the problem will become less complex by avoiding it.

ACTIVITY 8.1

Explain why we need a housing benefit system.

The current system

Housing benefit exists to enable people on low income to pay their rent. The amount that each individual claimant receives is determined by the actual rent they are charged. An individual on full income support will receive 100 per cent of their rent, whilst for those above this level the amount of support is reduced by 65 pence for every additional pound they earn. This situation can be altered by the household structure. Certain members of the household might be deemed to be non-dependants and thus assumed to be making a financial contribution to the household. As a result, entitlement to benefit is reduced. Likewise, certain groups such as lone parents and the elderly receive premiums which increase their entitlements.

Housing benefit is administered by local authorities, although the actual administration is split into two. Rent rebates paid to local authority tenants are accounted via the housing revenue account (HRA) (although the government has stated that it intends to take rent rebates out of the HRA) and rent allowances paid to private and housing association tenants administered through the General Fund. Until the introduction of ring fencing and HRA subsidy in 1989, a local authority could claim virtually all the cost of housing benefit back from central government. It can now claim 95 per cent of actual costs (including administration of the system), but rent rebate subsidy is offset against any negative subsidy entitlement on the HRA (see Chapter 4).

Housing benefit is not tenure neutral in its operation. The different tenures are treated differently for benefit purposes. Some measures apply to one tenure only, and not to the others. The effect is to create a complex system with differential incentives aimed at encouraging certain types of behaviour in one tenure but not in another.

Owner occupation

Housing benefit is intended to offset rent payments, and therefore owner occupiers are not eligible to receive support. As we saw in Chapter 7, financial supports to owner occupiers have traditionally taken the form of tax reliefs and thus have been dependent on the person having a sufficient income to pay tax.

However, owner occupiers in receipt of income support are entitled to receive some help with mortgage interest payments. This is limited to the first £100,000 of a mortgage and is available only after the applicant has been claiming income support for nine months. This limitation is aimed at encouraging owner occupiers to take out private insurance to cover their mortgage repayments in case of unemployment.

Private renting

Since 1996, housing benefit payments to private-sector tenants have been restricted by the local reference rent (LRR) system. This is where rents are restricted both by local average rent levels set by the rent officer and by household type. The rent officer may determine that housing benefit may be paid only up to a certain level based on what is reasonable for the area. In addition, payments to any particular household can be limited to what would be the rent for a property suitable to that household's needs.

This is an attempt to deal with so-called upmarketing, whereby households could choose to live in property larger than their needs warrant. The system aims to encourage households to reside only in suitably sized accommodation by restricting their rent payments accordingly. Prior to 1998, claimants received half the difference between the LRR and actual rent paid, but since then housing benefit has been payable only up to the LRR.

A further restriction which applies in the private rented sector is the so-called single room rent (SRR) restriction. This is where the housing benefit payments to childless single persons under 25 are restricted to the average cost of shared accommodation in the area. The reasons behind these restrictions and the effects that they have had are discussed in Chapter 6.

Housing associations

In some ways, housing associations have been in the most advantageous position with regard to housing benefit. The LRR system might apply to housing associations, but this is at the discretion of the relevant local authority for the area. In practice, most local authorities do not choose to apply the regulations and this means that they have fewer constraints on rent increases than either the private sector or local authorities themselves.

An indirect constraint is the inclusion of a rent formula as part of the bidding and performance review processes, which limits increases to 1 per cent above the rate of inflation (RPI + 1 per cent). The government proposed that from 2002, housing association rents would be limited to the rate of inflation plus 0.5 per cent. This will obviously have an impact on the cost of housing benefit, but it is noteworthy that this policy does not affect entitlements of individual tenants in the same way as do the LRR system or the SRR.

Local authorities

As with housing associations, there is no direct attempt to constrain the housing benefit entitlements of local authority tenants. But there are indirect controls that apply. These take the form of rent capping, whereby rent rebate subsidy is paid only at the rent guideline level. This acts as an incentive for local authorities to limit their rent increases as, on average, 65 per cent of their tenants are in receipt of housing benefit (see Table 8.1, p. 139). Local authority rent levels are so important because 60 per cent of housing benefit recipients are council tenants (DSS, 1997). Whilst this is a falling percentage, it does mean that changes to council rents have the biggest effect on the national housing benefit bill.

A more long-standing restriction on the cost of housing is the use of notional HRA surpluses to fund local housing benefit payments. Since 1994/5 the amount saved on housing benefit has outweighed the housing element of the HRA subsidy, meaning that government is effectively running council housing at a profit (see Chapter 4). The accumulated savings in housing benefit costs by government since 1990 are calculated at over £7 billion.

So, the manner in which housing benefit operates and the way government has set about trying to control housing benefit differs by sector. In the private rented sector it has tried to set rent ceilings. However, in the social rented sector it has attached controls to the capital subsidy system, rather than limiting entitlements.

The reason for this is that capital subsidies are easier for government to control as they involve direct payments to specific bodies according to definitive criteria. Government is able to change the criteria to suit its purposes and it has a reasonable hope of successfully achieving its aims. Thus it can reduce its liabilities by limiting rent rebate subsidy to a known increase rather than having to pay out according to locally determined rent increases. It is not possible to do this in the private rented sector simply because it does not provide any demand-side subsidies.

The problem for government is that the most controllable form of subsidy is subsidies on the supply side, but since the mid-1970s there has been a concerted shift towards demand-side housing subsidies. This has been because of a clear ideological imperative and a belief that local authorities were poor landlords (see the discussion on localism in Chapter 4). But this policy ran counter to general government policy under the Conservatives, which cut back on other demand-led subsidies such as student grants and free eye tests.

The differential treatment between tenures can have considerable consequences for other aspects of policy. For instance, one consequence of large-scale voluntary transfer (LSVT) was that transferring the housing stock from a local authority to a housing association meant that all the housing benefit could be reclaimed by the landlord. Between 1988 and 2000 over 450,00 dwellings have been transferred. As a result of this, in 1992 the Major government moved to limit LSVTs by establishing an annual quota and charging a 20 per cent levy on capital receipts.

ACTIVITY 8.2

Clearly outline the differences in the operation of housing benefit between the different tenures.

Also, the introduction of LRR and SRR has led some private landlords to refuse to house housing benefit claimants as they will not receive what the landlord considers the full rent (DETR, 1999). This will increase either street homelessness or the burden on social landlords.

Is housing benefit a problem?

The reform of housing benefit has been a key political issue since the mid-1990s. Since then both Conservative and Labour governments have tried to cut back on the growth of housing benefit. The problem can be traced back to a major change in rent policy enacted by the Housing Act 1988 and the Local Government and Housing Act 1989. The Conservative government reduced subsidies to social landlords and put a greater emphasis on rents as a source of income. But this merely shifted social landlords from a reliance on direct subsidy to a dependency on their tenants' entitlement to housing benefit.

Since 1991, housing benefit has grown by 11 per cent a year, compared to an average 4 per cent annual growth in the 1980s. In 1989/90 the total cost of housing benefit was £4.6 billion. By 1996/7, the last year of the Conservative government, it had increased to £12.2 billion (Wilcox, 2000). In subsequent years there has been a small decline, but with planned expenditure forecast to rise to £12.8 billion for the year 2001/2. This, however, is dependent on the state of the economy and the level of unemployment, as well as the effectiveness of the government's continued measures to control housing benefit. The growth in spending is shown in Table 8.2.

The small decline in housing benefit costs after 1997 has led some commentators to suggest that the problem is no longer serious. Much of the increase occurred in the first half of the 1990s, but since then falling

Table 8.2 *Growth of housing benefit expenditure, 1988–2002*

Year	£ billions
1988/9	4.0
1989/90	4.6
1990/1	5.7
1991/2	7.4
1992/3	9.0
1993/4	10.4
1994/5	11.1
1995/6	11.9
1996/7	12.2
1997/8	11.8
1998/9	11.7
1999/2000	11.8[a]
2000/1	12.2[a]
2001/2	12.8[a]

Sources: DSS HB factsheet (dss.gov.uk); Wilcox (2000)

Note: [a] Plans.

unemployment and attempts by successive governments to reduce rent levels in all sectors have brought this increase under control. This may account partly for why the Labour government felt able to delay any serious reform of the benefit system. Indeed, so long as the economy stays buoyant, and the government maintains its strong control over rent levels, then one can state that government might be able to limit the growth of housing benefit, and perhaps even stop real-term growth altogether.

However, the underlying structural problems with housing benefit remain. If unemployment were to rise, so would the cost of housing benefit, regardless of the rent policies enforced on landlords by government.

In any case, the issue is not entirely a financial one. The areas of concern about housing benefit do not just centre on the cost to the Exchequer. Britain already spends proportionately less on welfare than most of Europe (Hills, 1997). The cost of housing benefit is relatively small compared to the amount spent on education and health care. It accounts for only 12 per cent of social security spending and less than 3 per cent of total government spending.

It is not just cost that had concerned successive governments, but rather the effects that the housing benefit system has on tenants and landlords alike. The Blair government has stated that it considers welfare to be the 'cost of failure', in that individuals are being subsidised for being unproductive (DSS, 1998). They have argued that welfare policy ought to be more about assisting people back into work, rather than paying them to be idle. The government therefore saw an increasing welfare bill as the testament to failure. It would be more effective to use that money to help people find jobs and become independent and responsible for their own affairs. One of the objectives of the 2000 green paper was to promote 'self-dependence' (DETR, 2000a, p. 7). The concern, then, for the government was not merely that housing benefit was expensive, but that it was evidence of a failure of social policy.

There are other commentators who would go further and suggest that it is the system itself which actually creates a high and continuing level of demand (Coleman, 1992; Field, 1996; Marsland, 1996; Murray, 1996). Murray, for example, suggests that the benefit system has perverse incentives built into it which reward anti-social behaviour. Likewise Field, the former Minister for Welfare Reform, argued that a means-tested system such as housing benefit encourages dishonesty, idleness and a lack of thrift. This is because the payment of benefit is dependent on one's circumstances and thus there is no incentive to improve one's position. There may indeed be incentives to make one's position worse in order to maximise benefit entitlement. According to these critics, the issue is not about the cost of welfare benefits as much as being about welfare dependency and the waste of human potential.

Despite the government's refusal to undertake any reform of housing benefit, the government is quite clear what is wrong with the system (DETR, 2000a):

- Housing benefit is complex to deliver and to administer.
- Tenants don't understand the system and what they might be entitled to.
- The performance of local authorities (and their private subcontractors) in administering the system is inconsistent and inefficient.
- Administrative delay causes worry for tenants and might lead to eviction, as well as causing cash flow problems for landlords.
- Fraud is estimated as totalling £840 million per annum.
- Housing benefit deters people from taking jobs.
- Landlords exploit the system by charging high rents for poor-quality accommodation.
- Housing benefit takes responsibility away from tenants as they have little interest in their rent.

This appears quite a comprehensive list, certainly one that any government would need to act upon. But even this list tends to understate the nature of some of the problems. The green paper emphasises issues such as fraud and administrative delays because these are the issues that the green paper seeks to tackle. Fraud is indeed a serious issue, but much of it is possible because of the complexity of the system, allowing both landlords and tenants to take advantage of the system. Administrative reforms would help in this regard, as well as being necessary to speed up the assessment of claims. These problems are not, however, by any means the only, or even the main, problems with the housing benefit system. One can point to other issues which need attention in addition to those identified by the government.

First, tenants are treated differently in terms of age and tenure. This means that the system is not properly based on needs, but already makes value judgements on particular groups. One can question the validity of these assumptions and the equity of treating a 24-year-old differently from a 26-year-old.

Second, claimants receive premiums or have certain parts of their income disregarded depending on their circumstances, e.g. the elderly, carers, lone parents. This is a controversial issue, as some commentators, such as Murray (1996), have argued that the effect of these premiums is to encourage certain types of behaviour. This is known as *moral hazard*, where the attempt to deal with a problem increases its incidence. This is a controversial argument, but the government appeared to appreciate this point when it restricted the eligibility to lone parent premium for new claimants in 1997.

Field (1996) also argues that means testing is immoral. As households receive more benefits when their income is lowest, they have strong incentives to lie about their income and not to take up employment. Means testing, according to Field, is a disincentive to save, to be honest and to try to be independent. Furthermore, as means-tested benefits are targeted on the poorest, they help to create a divided society. Field argues for universal benefits in which all citizens receive something from the welfare state. According to Field, universal benefits create a sense of social cohesion where all parts of society believe they have a stake in the system and receive a benefit from it. He states that it is the middle classes who pay disproportionately more towards the cost of welfare and should receive something back. But means-tested benefits tend to go only to those who are not working and therefore not contributing through the tax system.

Third, one needs to consider the effect of the 65 per cent taper, whereby 65 pence of housing benefit is removed for every extra pound of income. This problem is compounded by the manner in which the tax and national insurance system also takes effect as income rises. Whilst the government is aware of this problem, and has reformed the tax and benefit systems to ensure that no one is worse off from working, this is still a problem which the government has not properly tackled.

Fourth, and I would suggest the biggest problem, is the ability of landlords to control housing benefit by having payments made directly to them (King, 2000). Housing benefit for all local authority tenants is paid directly to their landlord as part of HRA subsidy. Housing associations and private landlords have the right to direct payments if arrears are over eight weeks. However, many landlords insist on tenants signing payments over, or make it appear a condition of tenancy.

The ability of landlords to have payments made direct to them gives them considerable control over the benefit system. It is this practice which removes a sense of personal responsibility from tenants for their rent payments. An important area for reform is therefore to develop this sense of responsibility whilst at the same time breaking the hold that landlords have over benefit which allows them to create a link between rent levels and housing benefit. This problem is known as *producer capture* (Skidelsky, 1996), where a particular service is controlled by those managing it rather than those whom it is intended to benefit. The importance of this concept is that it questions just whom institutions and systems exist for: are they for the customers – in this case the tenants – or the producers? According to Skidelsky, the issue in the public sector is the ability of professionals – the producers – to control a service effectively for their own benefit. One could argue that the current housing benefit system is such that landlords, in both the social and private sectors, have been able to 'milk' the system by their ability to control rent levels. This 'milking' of the system is not fraud, but rather the entirely legal activity of maximising one's income by using the open nature of the housing benefit system.

The Conservative government attempted to deal with this with the introduction of local reference rents and the rent restrictions on social landlords we have already considered. The local reference rent system attempts to limit rents in the private sector to a reasonable level. Rent capping, as we saw in Chapter 4, is an attempt to limit local authority rent increases. Thus the belief of government has been that both social and private landlords have benefited unreasonably from housing benefit, and government has taken measures to contain them.

But it remains a problem still and will continue to be one so as long as landlords receive payments directly to themselves. The 2000 green paper partially recognises this problem and makes tentative proposals to make direct payments to private-sector tenants (see Chapter 6). However, it does not seem to consider the issue of irresponsibility a problem in the social housing sector, even though this is where the majority of housing benefit recipients reside.

The main arguments against ending direct payments are that rent arrears would increase, seriously affecting the finances of social and private landlords alike. Tenants, it is argued, would be tempted to use their housing benefit cash for other purposes and create an invidious choice between rent or items such as heating and children's shoes. Direct payments take away that temptation (although it does not help them to buy shoes!).

ACTIVITY 8.3

Why have landlords become so dependent on housing benefit? Is this a problem of the housing benefit system, or due to other factors such as the withdrawal of object subsidies?

There are, then, a considerable number of problems with the housing benefit system. In the next section I wish to look briefly at some of the proposals for reform and then to examine the government's reaction to these proposals.

Proposals for reform

The green paper, whilst writing off major reforms for a decade, does state a range of possible options for improving the administration of the system and reducing fraud. These changes include:

- information-sharing between DSS and local authorities;
- fixing benefit awards for a set period regardless of changed circumstances;
- introducing performance targets to cut fraud and error;
- establishing a national fraud hotline; and
- the possibility of disregarding minor changes to earnings so as to create incentives to work.

More significant are the proposals for limiting direct payments or cutting payments to certain landlords as discussed in Chapter 6. The green paper does discuss briefly the possibility of ending direct payments to landlords more generally, on the grounds that tenants might be ignorant of the actual rent charged and feel they have limited control over rent levels. However, whilst the government sees that this might have a limited role in the private rented sector (as discussed in Chapter 6), it dismisses a more general policy on the grounds that it would increase rent arrears and adversely affect landlords. It argues that '[t]he payment arrangements are administratively efficient for both local authorities and landlords' (DETR,

2000a, p. 120), and this appears to override any consideration of choice, despite this being one of the main themes of the green paper.

One reform that has been advocated by many is the reduction in the tapers by which housing benefit is reduced as income increases. The argument against the current 65 per cent taper is that it acts as a disincentive to work, particularly as it interacts with the tax and benefit system to create a marginal tax rate even higher than 65 per cent. The green paper rejects this proposal by arguing that it would be expensive and have only a marginal impact on work incentives. The government appears to be placing greater store on measures such as the working families tax credit which give low-income families a guaranteed minimum income.

The green paper discusses in some detail the advantages and disadvantages of a flat-rate level of benefit. Such a system would involve the abolition of housing benefit, which would be replaced entirely by a notional increase in income support to cover housing costs. The advantages of such a system include its simplicity to administer and ease of understanding. However, it has the disadvantage of not taking into account variations in individual circumstances. Accordingly, the green paper concludes that a fully flat-rate scheme 'does not look an attractive option' (DETR, 2000a, p. 118).

'Shopping incentives'

The preferred option appears to be an amended form of flat-rate payment which incorporates a so-called shopping incentive. Kemp (2000) argues that the main weakness of the current housing benefit system is that 'the amount of rent for which households are liable – and therefore, the amount of housing benefit to which they are entitled – is to some degree determined by the housing choices that they make' (p. 2). This creates a potential moral hazard problem, in that households can commit themselves to high rents knowing that the benefit system will cover the cost. Kemp argues that this problem is made worse by the fact that many recipients have all their rent paid for them. The idea of introducing 'shopping incentives' is to ensure that households become more sensitive to rent levels.

His proposal would involve 80 per cent of a household's rent being met by housing benefit, with the remaining 20 per cent being made up by the tenant from their income support. Income support would be increased to

ACTIVITY 8.4

Who has most to benefit from the reform of housing benefit?

allow this, but through a flat-rate increase worth 20 per cent of average housing costs for the area and household size. This would give the tenants some incentive to 'shop around' as they would keep any portion of the difference between the actual rent and their increased income support payment. The green paper suggests that income support could be uprated by 25 per cent of average housing costs to provide an extra margin of affordability. However, as I have stressed often enough in this chapter, any reform is some way off.

Summary

In this chapter I have:

● explored the nature of the housing benefit system and how it differs according to tenure;

● discussed whether fundamental reform is required and what reforms have been proposed; and

● considered the reasons why serious reform has been postponed

Further reading

Housing benefit, as I have shown, is fearsomely complicated. An excellent guide to the regulations is provided by Zebedee and Ward (annually). Their guide is updated annually to take into account changes in the regulations. Kemp (1998, 2000) offers a good discussion of the debate for the reform of housing benefit, and Kemp (1997) puts the debate into an international context. For an argument about the abolition of housing benefit, see King (1999). For a general discussion on the debate about the future of welfare, try Hills (1997), and see King and Oxley (2000) for a discussion of how this debate relates to housing more generally.

9 After 1997: something new or more of the same?

- The changes made in housing finance policy since 1997
- Does the 1997 election represent continuity or change with the policies of the 1980s and 1990s?
- Key trends in housing finance over the past twenty-five years

Introduction

In this chapter I want specifically to look at the policies of the Labour government elected in 1997. In particular I wish to consider those proposals in the 2000 housing green paper (DETR, 2000a) that are likely to affect housing finance. Accordingly, this chapter will consider issues such as stock transfer, sustainable owner occupation, rent restructuring, as well as the reluctance to adopt a comprehensive approach to housing benefit reform.

Of course, I have already considered several of these issues in the previous chapters. Housing benefit is a crucial issue that affects all rented tenures, and hence deserved a chapter to itself. My aim here, though, is to try to deal with current policy in the round. There is a purpose to this, which is to show that there is a considerable degree of continuity between the policies pursued before and after 1997. The Labour government is merely continuing with the general trends in housing finance policy which began in the 1970s and were carried on by the Conservatives in the 1980s and 1990s.

These issues are important to the larger picture I have tried to paint in this book. Housing has increasingly been subsumed into larger priorities such as the control of public spending and the extension of market-based and choice models of provision. This could be achieved only by increasing the level of central control over housing providers. The key issues I wish to consider in this chapter all fit into this model of extending central control to achieve more market-based systems of provision.

This chapter will lead on to a discussion of key themes in housing finance since the 1970s. My aim is to show a considerable degree of consistency between Conservative and Labour governments, in terms of support for owner occupation as the aspirational tenure (DoE, 1995; DETR, 2000a) and a distrust of social landlords, who therefore need to be controlled to ensure they fulfil the aims of government. I shall identify four themes that have characterised housing finance policy since the 1970s. These are:

- owner occupation;
- centralisation;
- liberalisation; and
- individualisation.

ACTIVITY 9.1

List the important financial elements in the housing green paper *Quality and Choice: A Decent Home for All* (DETR, 2000a).

My aim in this chapter is to show that the new policies developed by the Labour administration are merely a continuation and development of these core themes. Therefore, whilst the green paper might be superseded by events, it still fits within a general pattern of policy-making.

Continuity or change?

All governments like to suggest that they represent a radical departure from their predecessors, and the Blair government elected in 1997 has been no different. It has been quick to try to identify itself with progress and modernisation and the pursuit of an agenda that is different from both the Conservatives' and that of previous Labour administrations (Blair, 1998; Brown, 1999a). As was discussed in Chapter 2, the Blair government has claimed to be developing a Third Way approach, between traditional socialism and Thatcherite individualism.

But in many ways the attitude of the Blair government to housing is similar to that of the Conservatives. Despite the fact that the Labour Party has traditionally been more favourable towards local authorities, it made a manifesto commitment to maintain the Major government's spending plans and priorities for its first two years in office. In addition, it has retained the capping of local authority expenditure and income, despite arguing against the measure whilst in opposition. Local authorities have been given more resources since 1997, but it is still central government that determines the priorities and sets the performance standards by which local authorities are to be judged. Housing associations are still prey to Housing Corporation regulation. Indeed, the rent restructuring proposals included in the 2000 green paper suggest an increased preparedness to intervene in the affairs of what are supposed to be private bodies. It is not unreasonable to suggest, then, that there has been no lessening of central regulation and control since 1997, even though the rhetoric used by government might have changed.

The attitude of the Labour government can be demonstrated by reiterating a quotation from the former housing minister, Hilary Armstrong (see also the discussion in Chapter 4). In 1998 she stated:

> It's very much about a local choice – but local choices have consequences. The consequences may mean it is much harder for me to argue with the chancellor that the money is being well spent and he should keep the flow going.
>
> (quoted in Blake, 1998, p. 20)

This quotation offers considerable insight into the government's thinking. Choice is being promoted, in terms of allocations and between tenures, but households and housing providers are being offered choice only on the government's terms. Proposals such as resource accounting and the single capital pot might have the proclaimed aim of enhancing local autonomy. But the government is always there to tell housing organisations what they should do with their autonomy. Moreover, there is always the 'big stick' in the form of bodies such as the Housing Inspectorate and the Audit Commission to enforce the government's view.

In some ways the Blair government has taken centralised control further than its Conservative predecessors. As Jenkins (1995) predicted (see Chapter 4), the Conservatives developed a control mechanism which would prove amenable to the more activist approach of Labour administrations. Even though Labour argued against many of the specific measures whilst in opposition, these controls have remained largely untouched. They have subsequently been beefed up by the introduction of the Housing Inspectorate, the use of business planning and the Best Value regime.

It is instructive that the government now sees local authority housing as a 'national programme' and believes that 'assumed surpluses in authorities' housing accounts should be retained within housing and redistributed through a pooling mechanism' (DETR press release 370, 23 May 2000).

Much of the government's housing proposals since 1997 can be seen as *institutionalising* the trends in housing since the 1970s. Thus resource accounting and the shift in emphasis from credit approvals to a major repairs allowance (see Chapter 4) institutionalise the fact that local authorities are landlords and not developers. Likewise, the rent restructuring proposals in the green paper extend central government control over housing association rents and further entrench their *parastatal* position (see Chapter 5). Nowhere is this extension of the Conservative agenda so prevalent as in the 2000 housing green paper.

Quality and choice: the 2000 housing green paper

After nearly three years of Labour government the 2000 housing green paper appeared to offer a clear signal of where housing policy is headed. It was awaited particularly to see how policy was going to change from that of the Conservatives. The government itself was in no doubt, calling the green paper 'the first comprehensive review of housing for 23 years' (DETR, 2000a, p. 5).

However, what was immediately noticeable about the green paper was how much of the Conservative agenda – stock transfer, the support for owner occupation, the right to buy, the use of private finance – remained as the cornerstone of the proposals. Much of the green paper appears to build on the Conservatives' legacy and to take it a stage further.

As commentators have argued, the proposals in the 2000 green paper might be comprehensive, but they are not radical. As *Roof Briefing* has stated, 'This is a managerial rather than ideological green paper, producing an avalanche of new procedures for every nook and cranny of the housing sector. But the big picture remains the same' (*Roof Briefing*, no. 39, April 2000, p. 2). It goes on to suggest that the green paper 'will not herald a sea change like the 1980 Act's right to buy or the 1988 Act's deregulation of private renting and switch to private finance' (p. 2). Thus the Labour government is accused of lacking a vision for housing and for adopting a managerial approach which builds on the policies of its predecessors.

Thus despite frequent references in the green paper to the Conservatives' underinvestment and poor policy, many of the policies developed between

1979 and 1997 remain intact. No major changes to the right to buy are envisaged; housing benefit is to remain in its current state for at least the next decade (despite this being one of the main justifications for the 'comprehensive' review in the first place); and no changes are planned to assured and assured shorthold tenancies. Moreover, the main idea of the Major government, namely the transferring of council housing into the private sector, is taken up as a vehicle for dealing with the purported backlog in capital repairs and to improve housing management. The green paper envisages the transfer of up to 200,000 dwellings per year, which would see the virtual end of council housing in fifteen years, leaving local authorities as strategic enablers only. The idea that local authorities should be the disbursers and monitors of contracts and not directly involved in provision was very much one developed by radical Conservative politicians such as the former Secretary of State for the Environment, Nicholas Ridley.

Even more surprising is the admission in the green paper on at least three occasions that 'Most people are well housed' (see pp. 7, 15, 20). This again hardly indicates a huge discrepancy between Conservative and Labour governments. It suggests either that the Conservatives were largely successful in their housing policies, or that both governments are equally complacent when it comes to housing. In either case, it limits the possibility for moral outrage on the part of the Blair government. It perhaps suggests that the government does not see housing as its biggest political priority and that it can live with the legacy of the Conservatives on this issue.

In terms of positive proposals in the green paper, many of these can be seen as developments of existing themes. For example, the proposal for a *Starter Home Initiative*, offering subsidies to key workers in high-demand areas, is an extension of the Conservatives' support for owner occupation. Indeed, the green paper demonstrates a continuation of the policy adopted by the Conservatives in 1993 of supporting owner occupation at the margins, but of concentrating on economic stability. The green paper states, 'The main contribution the Government can make to sustainable homeownership is a robust economy in all parts of the country and a strong system of consumer protection' (DETR, 2000a, p. 30). As part of this policy of non-intervention the Blair government has continued with the phasing out of mortgage interest tax relief. Again this is a case of carrying a Conservative initiative to its logical conclusion.

Another proposal is the introduction of greater choice into housing allocations by using customer-led lettings systems. These systems would allow applicants a greater choice in the type and location of dwellings compared to the traditional points-based waiting-list systems. However, one could also suggest that choice in allocations is merely a logical development of the policies of liberalisation and individualisation introduced by the Conservatives. Instead of market-testing housing through Compulsory Competitive Tendering, the product is now to be actively tested by offering customers a choice. If this policy is allowed to develop to its full extent, it will show most graphically which dwelling types and locations are popular and at what rent levels.

The proposals to restructure social housing rents can also be seen as the continuation of Conservative policy. The Conservatives, having unleashed considerable rent increases in 1989, sought to restrict rents from 1996 onwards. They attempted to achieve some compromise whereby rents were affordable, yet where they could still ensure that private finance and low subsidy levels remained viable. The proposals to restrict rent increases and to ensure comparability between social landlords are aimed at having the same effect. The trend in subsidy up to 2004 may be upwards, but this only returns subsidy to its levels in the mid-1990s. However, what rent restructuring will allow is for central government to exert much greater influence over the income and expenditure of social landlords to a level not contemplated by the Conservatives.

Why continuity and not change?

I have demonstrated that there are clear continuities between the Conservative and Labour governments. It is interesting to speculate why this state of affairs has come about. I would like to suggest that there might be three reasons.

First, any new government, despite its rhetoric, has to make use of existing institutions and policy instruments. The Blair government could not wish away the changes made since 1979, but had to work with them and to transform them slowly, whilst at the same time maintaining a reasonable level of service. The 'year zero' approach of demolishing all existing institutions and building from scratch is not a tenable one. Indeed, it is instructive that the main structural changes to social policy under the Conservatives took place after the third election victory in 1987 rather than when they were first elected in 1979. Likewise, it is unreasonable to expect the Blair government to have transformed social policy in less than three years. A variation of this view is that the Thatcherite reforms had gone so far that they were impossible to reverse.

There is some merit in this argument, but it is important to realise that the 2000 green paper is a set of proposals purportedly based on 'the first comprehensive review of housing for 23 years' (DETR, 2000a, p. 5). The green paper is intended not as an interim measure, but as the result of fundamental thinking on the future of housing policy, and I would suggest that the significant continuity of policy should be seen in that light. One must presume that the Labour government found that a lot wasn't broke and therefore didn't need fixing.

This relates to the second possible reason for continuity. Might it not be that the Blair government is in fact a conservative one? It has maintained many of the Conservative Party's policies because it agrees with them ideologically on the basis of their fiscal conservatism and support for individual choice and opportunity. If the ideological divide between the Conservative and Labour governments is not wide, then it is not surprising that there is a continuity of policy.

But this begs the question of whether the Thatcher and Major administrations were indeed properly conservative, or whether, as Jenkins (1995) has argued, their centralist policies were more demonstrative of the Labour tradition of planning and intervention. Unfortunately, this debate goes beyond the scope of the present discussion, except to say that there has been no shortage of critics from the right who would concur with Jenkins' analysis, particularly of the Major government (Hitchens, 1999; Williams, 1998). In any case, the Blair government's agenda does appear to overlap considerably with that of the Conservatives and hence that government has continued many of the initiatives and intends to extend some of them further. In housing policy terms at least, both main political parties are playing to the same constituency. It might not be coincidence that the word 'choice' features in the titles of both the 1995 white paper and the 2000 green paper. Housing policy is still centred around owner occupation as the 'aspirational' tenure that most households have or would choose. Government cannot ignore social housing, but it is less politically important than those welfare goods such as health care, pensions and education provided on a universal basis.

This leads on to the third reason for the continuity in policy. It might be because the Conservatives' policies were relatively successful and that politicians, with an acute sense of the popular, will naturally seek to continue with them. Owner occupation, despite the recession in the

ACTIVITY 9.2

Discuss why fundamental change in housing policy is so difficult to achieve.

1990s, remains popular and thus politicians are likely to support it. With regard to social housing, centralisation of policy-making has ensured a level of control over institutions that the current (Blair) government finds as congenial as its predecessors.

Four themes in housing finance

Having argued that there has been considerable continuity in housing policy since the late 1970s, I now wish to discuss what I consider to be the main trends shared by the Conservatives and Labour.

The first and perhaps most obvious theme is the promotion and support of owner occupation as a tenure of choice. The second theme is one I have stressed consistently throughout this book, that of centralisation. The liberalisation of institutions forms the third theme of housing policy and consists of the introduction of private finance, market testing and the transferring of housing stock. Lastly, we have seen the individualisation of housing policy, partly through a concentration on owner occupation, but also through a shift away from supply-side subsidies and towards demand-side subsidies such as housing benefit and mortgage interest tax relief.

These four trends are, of course, intertwined and related to each other, but in other respects they contradict one another. Individualisation relates to the pursuit of owner occupation, but then centralisation clearly militates against the pursuit of individual choice and independence. However, despite the linkages and apparent contradictions, these four strands are distinct and worthy of separate consideration.

Owner occupation

Whilst the Conservative government elected in 1979 was not the first to promote owner occupation, its support for this tenure was certainly more manifest than that of any previous government had been. Indeed, I would suggest that the particular importance of the Thatcher government was the manner in which it *depoliticised* housing policy by effectively privatising it. Several commentators on the right, such as Green (1993), have argued that one aim of social and public policy should be to 'return' these policies to civil society, and thus take them out of the political realm. The Conservatives saw that housing was particularly amenable to this privatisation, in that, regardless of who pays for it, it is enjoyed privately.

More particularly, housing is both predictable and understandable. We know that we need housing and will continue to do so. Moreover, we can understand how that need can be met (King, 1998). Housing has thus proved to be an amenable area for privatisation, particularly in comparison to other welfare goods such as education and health. This privatisation has involved the use of private finance for housing associations and the transferring of local authority stock, but it is also manifested by the encouragement of owner occupation, whereby individual households provide their own housing.

The most obvious example of government support for owner occupation was the right to buy. The right to buy can be seen as the most influential housing policy of the 1979–97 period, in that it had a fundamental impact on housing structures, albeit merely speeding up already discernible trends towards greater owner occupation. The significance of the policy was in terms of both the boost it gave to owner occupation and the effect it had on social housing providers left with less affluent tenants and a housing stock reduced in terms of both quantity and quality.

The debate over the right to buy identified the crucial divide in housing policy between left and right in the 1980s and into the 1990s. For the left, it showed a disregard for the needs of the poor and a deliberate attempt to destroy a key basis for working-class solidarity (Somerville and Knowles, 1991). For those on the right, it was an attempt to liberate individuals from state dependency (Saunders, 1990). It also showed a key division in terms of thinking about housing. The left saw the problem in collective terms. They looked at the effects on the stock of social housing (and those organisations that owned it) and on those groups who were now denied access or were experiencing a residualised service. The right, however, along with the Conservative government itself, saw the virtue of the right to buy as individualising the monolithic nature of housing provision, by allowing individuals to achieve their aspirations. Thus the left tended to concentrate on the collective effects whilst the right trumpeted the individual gains. In this way the controversy over the right to buy manifested the key ideological differences between left and right in this period.

But this debate also demonstrated another important facet about the political significance of housing. Throughout this period, and despite a huge increase in official homelessness in the late 1980s, housing became a significant political issue only when the focus was on owner occupation. The right to buy caused considerable controversy and indeed became a key factor in the heavy defeat of the Labour Party in 1983 after the party had made a commitment to repurchase former council stock. But housing came to the top of the political agenda only when the housing market was either overheating, as occurred in the late 1980s, or when the boom turned into a major slump in the early 1990s.

In dealing with this slump, the Conservatives were quite prepared to use funding allocated for social housing in order to enhance owner occupation. This was seen in the shift in priorities of the Housing Corporation's Approved Development Programme (ADP) towards ownership initiatives, and the use of ADP funds to purchase empty dwellings in the owner-occupied sector to try to shore up the housing market after Britain left the Exchange Rate Mechanism (ERM) in 1992.

Whilst much of the unpopularity of the Major government after 1992 was doubtless due to the humiliating departure from the ERM, as I pointed out in Chapter 7 it is interesting to speculate how far that unpopularity was magnified by the depression in the housing market. The problem for the Conservatives was that they had so closely associated themselves with owner occupation that they could not help but be seriously affected by a prolonged housing slump. The housing boom of the 1980s, helped by the financial deregulation allowing banks and building societies to compete with each other within a liberalised market, created consumer confidence and a sense of well-being which the Conservatives were quick to capitalise on. However, once the booming housing market collapsed, the Conservatives were not able to disassociate themselves from owner occupation. Thus, whilst the policy of supporting owner occupation had great clarity and resonated with a significant part of the electorate, this very clarity served to harm the Conservatives once housing became to be seen more as a liability than as an asset.

After 1993, policy towards owner occupation changed somewhat. Instead of supporting the tenure through subsidies and incentives, the new Chancellor of the Exchequer, Kenneth Clarke, shifted towards a policy of stability. As a result, tax relief on mortgage interest was phased out.

The Chancellor argued that the best support to the tenure was not through specific tax reliefs but through stable economic conditions and low inflation, which allows for low interest rates. This policy recognised that factors such as unemployment and job security were more significant than subsidies in creating a sustaining and active housing market. This policy has allowed a steady recovery in owner occupation throughout the 1990s.

As we have seen, the 2000 green paper leaves untouched the right to buy and suggests that sustainable owner occupation is to be supported. As we saw in Chapter 7, the government feels the best way to achieve sustainability is economic stability. Thus the Blair government intends to continue with the policy initiated by Kenneth Clarke in 1993.

Centralisation

We have discussed the centralisation of housing policy at some length, particularly in the chapters on social housing (see Chapters 2–5). As we have seen, centralisation was considered necessary because of the distinctive imperative of the Thatcher government, which saw the prioritisation of public spending over any notion of housing need. Partly this was because of the importance of choice and independence in Conservative ideology, but it was also because of a more general belief that public spending and certain institutions were out of control. Of course, the more controls were exerted, the greater the political opposition, which, from the government's perspective, merely necessitated a high level of control and intervention.

Conservative centralisation became manifest in the attempt to break up local authorities' housing stock with the expressed aim of giving tenants the choice and opportunity of owner occupation. In time the policy developed through the use of private finance, and 'market testing' initiatives such as Housing Action Trusts, Tenants' Choice and Compulsory Competitive Tendering. However, these policies could be achieved only through the centralisation of power and control in Whitehall and Westminster. None of these policies developed because of a groundswell of opinion from tenants, or indeed because local authorities themselves considered them to be needed. They derived from the central government's perception of the role of local authorities and the needs of tenants.

One can dispute whether the Conservatives ever achieved the objectives they set themselves of fully controlling social housing. Indeed, the fact that they had to intervene at regular intervals and undertake major overhauls of policy in 1980, 1987 and 1996 indicates that they were not able to sustain any real level of control over time. However, they certainly took to themselves considerable powers in order to give themselves the greatest opportunity. In relation to the financial regime controlling local authorities, central government gained permanent leverage over income and expenditure, and thus rent levels and the quality of service provided through the Local Government and Housing Act 1989. With regard to housing associations, the reforms to housing association grant introduced in the Housing Act 1988 have destroyed much of their community orientation and led them towards a more commercial culture *without* lessening their dependence on central government funding.

What the Conservatives were able to achieve, then, was a series of mechanisms which effectively turned local authorities into local branches doing the bidding of central government, leaving housing associations limited access to public funds for new building so long as they met government priorities.

Jenkins (1995) made the point that not only did centralisation diminish local autonomy and diversity, replacing it within standardised solutions, it also established a set of mechanisms that could be taken up by a government more amenable to intervention and central planning. Perhaps inadvertently, a Conservative government had developed the framework of a socialist planning system. The Blair government when taking office in 1997 therefore already had at its command the tools to control and mould housing and social policy in a way that the Labour governments of the 1960s and 1970s never had. Of course, whether it chooses to exercise that power for any ends that are remotely socialist is another matter.

Liberalisation

The centralisation of policy has been an implicit imperative, in that it was never an openly stated objective of government (although the Labour government's argument that social housing is a national programme perhaps makes the trend more explicit). Indeed, much of the rhetoric of the Conservatives consisted of the very reverse. The Conservatives' aim, consistent with their general policy of privatisation, was to liberalise processes and to deregulate, allowing market processes to influence policy outcomes. Likewise, the Blair government has promoted decentralisation as a key aim in terms of its constitutional reforms, but also with regard to local government. Resource accounting, for instance, is described by the government as offering greater autonomy to local authorities.

This may appear to be an example of hypocrisy at the very highest level, in that government is claiming to liberalise and to increase autonomy when in fact it is doing the opposite. However, there is something of a logic to it. Whilst policies such as the right to buy might have been popular with tenants and the electorate generally, they could be achieved only in the face of opposition from local authorities and the housing profession. Other policies such as Tenants' Choice and Housing Action Trusts had likewise to be imposed on reluctant local housing organisations. Thus the Conservative government could not necessarily rely on the co-operation of local authorities to implement its policies. It needed to be able to force local authorities to do its bidding, and to continually monitor them to guarantee compliance. Liberalisation and deregulation could be undertaken only through a policy of the 'pacification' of hostile local providers.

Of course, the practical logic of this scenario does not limit the contradiction involved in 'forcing' individuals and organisations to be 'free'. The Conservatives appeared to believe that certain lower layers of government were problematical, whilst central government was immune to the problems.

Nevertheless, there have been genuine attempts to liberalise and deregulate housing systems. Attempts were made to privatise provision, such as the right to buy. But where this was not possible, the aim was to introduce market disciplines.

Thus throughout the 1990s the level of central discretion allowed in allocating capital finance for local authorities through the housing investment programme system process was increased, and the importance of needs indicators consequently reduced. The aim here was to allow for measures of relative efficiency to be taken into account rather than local needs. The idea was to encourage local authorities to compete with each other on the basis of expected performance rather than being able to set their own agendas according to local conditions. Running alongside this shift towards performance monitoring was the imposition of Compulsory Competitive Tendering (CCT) to 'market test' the efficiency of local authorities' housing services. These measures introduced commercial disciplines into local authorities and allowed for comparisons to be made on relative efficiency. Whilst the Blair government abolished CCT, it has replaced it with Best Value, which has a similar aim of ensuring improvement in performance by continual comparison of best practice. Resource accounting is also aimed at ensuring that local authorities are more commercially orientated.

An increasingly significant example of liberalisation has been the transfer of local authority stock to alternative landlords. As we have seen, the 2000 green paper (DETR, 2000a) envisages a significant increase in the pace of transfer. Additionally, the government is actively pursuing the alternatives of arm's-length companies and the Private Finance Initiative as means to lever in private finance to the municipal sector.

Liberalisation has also occurred in the housing association sector. The Housing Act 1988 attempted to redesignate housing associations as part of an independent rented sector along with private landlords. Rent controls were to be abolished and statutory tenancies replaced by contractual assured tenancies weighted more in favour of landlords. Landlords now had greater control over rent levels and were no longer prey to the right to buy. These changes were necessary for housing associations as public-sector grants were reduced and replaced with the need to raise private finance. Grant rates have been reduced from levels of around 80 per cent in 1989 to a national average of 54 per cent in 2000, but with many associations building with grant rates of below 25 per cent (we should note here that this trend is reversing, with the grant rate increased to 60 per cent in 2001).

The use of private finance was compounded by the encouragement of competitive bidding for Housing Corporation funding. Housing associations were given the grant rate and total cost indicators as a guide to bidding. But one criterion is that bids are judged on the basis of the amount of public funding required. This encouraged associations to limit their call on public funding to enhance the possibility of success in the bidding process.

These changes to housing association finance, one structural and the other procedural, have dramatically altered the ethos and organisation of housing associations, shifting them away from their traditional charitable basis and welfare orientation and towards a more commercial framework. However, it is important to note that housing associations have thrived in the decade since private finance was introduced.

As a result of these changes, the criteria for efficiency were based on value-for-money criteria, rather than on alleviating housing need or levels of service provision. Again, though, this demonstrates a paradox in housing policy, in that public funding is dependent upon whether an organisation can demonstrate private-sector disciplines. This has meant that bureaucratic controls are being used to administer commercialisation, and, as a result, the major change has been a heightened dependence on central regulation. Change has been motivated not on the basis of choice for the 'customer', but as a top-down exercise in organisational manipulation.

A further important liberalisation was the deregulation of the mortgage market, allowing both building societies and banks to diversify and compete against each other. The effect was an increase in competition in the mortgage market. This might have helped fuel the housing boom of the late 1980s, but it has also led to the introduction of more flexible mortgage instruments. Likewise, the removal of rent controls and security of tenure in the private sector has seen a liberalisation of private renting leading to a marginal revival in the fortunes of private landlords.

Individualisation

Perhaps the largest structural change in housing policy since 1979 has been the shift away from object subsidies towards subject subsidies (see Chapters 2 and 3). In 1979 over two-thirds of subsidy was paid to housing providers. These sums were aimed at allowing local authorities and housing associations to provide new additional housing at subsidised rents, and to maintain their existing stock. The remaining third of housing expenditure was paid out in the form of tax relief to owner occupiers and rent rebates.

However, the balance between object and subject subsidies shifted dramatically in the 1980s and 1990s. By the end of the Conservatives' period in office, the situation had changed even further, with spending on housing providers accounting for only 21.9 per cent of housing expenditure. Thus, despite a decline in MITR from its peak in 1990, demand-side subsidies in 1996/7 accounted for 78.1 per cent of housing expenditure. Indeed, in 1996/7, housing benefit itself (at £12.2 billion) was very nearly three times the amount spent on general housing expenditure (£4.1 billion). What the 1979–97 period saw, then, was a re-ordering of housing expenditure, with a significant fall in government support to housing providers, but much of that funding shifting to individual tenants and owners.

This change in the balance between object and subject subsidies implied a change in the purpose of housing subsidies. Instead of subsidy being used to increase supply, it was now aimed at bolstering demand. The belief was that there was enough housing for the number of households in the country. What was therefore at issue was not the quantity of housing, but whether all households could gain access to housing of sufficient quality. It is therefore the issues of access and quality that are at the centre of the shift from object to subject subsidies.

This theme perhaps most directly relates to the ideological imperative of the Conservatives towards independence and choice. This was to be furthered not through subsidies to housing providers, but through individual subsidies to households allowing them some choice in determining what and where they lived. Hence the 1987 white paper's favourable discussion of tax relief alongside the need to curb the purportedly over-generous subsidies to social housing (DoE, 1987).

However, what became very clear in the 1990s was that the pursuit of individual choice, through the use of subject subsidies such as housing benefit, conflicted with the centralisation of policy. In most other areas of social and public policy the Conservatives moved in a different direction. They curtailed open-ended demand-led commitments, such as mandatory grants for students in higher education, preferring instead to rely on direct Treasury funding to organisations. The reason for this was that the Treasury could apply a much greater level of control over expenditure through the supply side than through the demand side. The individualisation of housing finance was a move in the opposite direction and, indeed, had the effect of making housing expenditure harder to control. The government cannot control the numbers of claimants eligible, nor until the late 1990s has it been able to control rent levels upon which benefit payments depend.

As we have seen in the discussion on housing benefit in Chapter 8, this open-ended policy was changed in 1996 and an increasing level of control has been placed on housing benefit and rent levels, culminating in the Labour government's proposals for rent restructuring. What this suggests is that where the four themes conflict there are clear winners. In particular, the determination to control activity from the centre has consistently been favoured where it clashes with individualisation or liberalisation.

I believe that there is a clear connection between housing policies undertaken before and after the 1997 election. There may be some changes in rhetoric and changes in the balance of funding. Yet these are marginal compared to the far greater continuity shown in the four themes discussed in this chapter.

Of course, we shouldn't really be surprised by this. The dominance of owner occupation is now such that any other form of provision is likely only ever to have a marginal influence. No government could successfully challenge this dominance, even if it wanted to. We therefore have a new consensus in housing policy, formed around owner occupation as the tenure of choice and supported by a centralised system of policy-making aimed at maintaining political control over social housing. Since 1997 the Labour government has not sought to change this, but rather it has institutionalised the process.

ACTIVITY 9.3

List what you consider to be the most important housing finance policies of the past twenty years (this will check whether you've read the book!).

Summary

In this chapter I have:

- considered the changes made to housing finance policy since 1997;

- suggested that there is a considerable degree of continuity between the Conservative (Thatcher and Major) and Labour (Blair) governments;

- sought reasons for this continuity; and

- identified four key themes in housing finance policy over the past twenty-five years, namely, owner occupation, centralisation, liberalisation and individualisation.

Further reading

The key aim of this chapter has been to pick out the themes in previous chapters, and so these previous chapters are essential to the discussion in this chapter. However, an obvious further reference is to the 2000 housing green paper, *Quality and Choice* (DETR, 2000a).

A book that looks at the issue of continuity and change in housing, albeit with the emphasis on the change, is that edited by Brown (1999a), which considers a Third Way approach to housing.

⑩ Where to now?

Introduction

In this concluding chapter I wish to consider briefly where housing finance policy seems to be heading over the next few years. Of course, much of this discussion is speculative. One of the consequences of taking a political approach is that one must be aware of the unforeseen. I am not suggesting that I am capable of seeing into the future. Rather I am confident that the unexpected will occur and that this will dramatically alter the direction of policy. Governments lose elections, economies nosedive into recession and households have the bad manners to do what governments don't want them to do. Any or all of these could blow the government's policies off course.

I would, however, like to suggest that there are a number of possible future scenarios which we can usefully consider here. In particular I want to look at the following issues:

- Are we about to see the end of council housing?
- Is the current system of housing benefit sustainable?
- What impact will rent restructuring have on housing associations?

There is a danger that the discussion that follows may quickly become irrelevant if the government changes or if other unforeseen events intervene. However, the risk is worth taking in the sense that these issues are at the forefront of housing finance policy and are unlikely to go away even if the government changes.

This is because, as I have tried to show in the previous chapter, these issues fit in with the core themes of housing finance policy over the past

ACTIVITY 10.1

What do you consider to be the most important housing finance issues over the next decade? Pick out at least three key issues and give reasons why you think they will be so important.

two decades. My view is that a change of government will not dramatically alter the direction of policy; the Labour government is not doing anything drastically different from its predecessors, and there are no grounds to suggest that a future Conservative government will change these priorities.

The end of council housing?

The 2000 green paper outlines some important proposals that could have far-reaching effects for council housing in particular. The government proposes to increase the scale of stock transfers to up to 200,000 a year. It also proposes the establishment of arm's-length companies to manage local authority housing, with the best-performing companies given increased powers to borrow. The government is also carrying out pilots for the Private Finance Initiative (PFI) that would involve private-sector management of the stock, even though it would technically remain a public asset.

These proposals can be seen as offering a range of alternatives for local authorities. Some might choose stock transfer as the best option, but the history of LSVT has shown that this is perhaps suitable only for relatively small authorities with limited debt and stock of a generally good quality. This position might change, as now several larger urban authorities such as Birmingham and Coventry are taking the transfer route.

However, the government still anticipates that there will be a considerable amount of local authority housing by 2005 (*Roof*, vol. 25, no. 3, May/June 2000, pp. 18–21). Indeed, it is likely that stock transfer will not be an option for the worst-quality stock, simply because it won't be attractive to the private sector as an investment. Therefore the other vehicles the government is developing – arm's-length companies and the PFI – might be more suitable alternatives. They involve the private sector, but the perceived level of risk might be reduced by the continuation of central government subsidy. In the case of arm's-length companies they will have additional borrowing rights only if they have been rated excellent by the Best Value process and are fulfilling the government's requirements on rents and lettings. The other advantage from the government's perspective is that arm's-length companies and PFI partnerships would still remain under the local authority rent rebate regime, allowing for the continued capture of rent surpluses limiting the government's rent rebate liability (see Chapter 4).

There is, though, some apparent conflict in pursuing mass stock transfer on the one hand and arm's-length companies on the other. One encourages the stock out of the sector, whilst the other makes it easier for the best-performing authorities to put off transfer. The key to this apparent contradiction may well be that the green paper (DETR, 2000a) envisages that only a small number of authorities will be able to pursue the option of increased borrowing. This promise of increased borrowing might therefore be best seen in political terms as a means of encouraging local authorities to perform well, whilst allowing the government to suggest that they have an alternative to stock transfer.

What is apparent, however, is that past attempts to devise vehicles to use private finance, such as Housing Action Trusts, Tenants' Choice, Housing Investment Trusts and local housing companies, have foundered. The only successful means of injecting private finance so far has been through stock transfer. This might be because stock transfer is a much more straightforward process, one that is understandable for councillors, housing professionals, tenants and financial institutions. The other vehicles that have been devised have all been complex and difficult to understand. It may well be that arm's-length companies and the PFI will go the same way, as ideas that had potential but which failed the tests of simplicity and understandability. In any case, I would speculate that it is doubtful that both increased stock transfer and these other vehicles using private finance can co-exist. Time, however, may very well prove me wrong.

However, even if mass stock transfer does become the norm, this does not mean the end of *social housing*. If council housing is transferred to new landlords, it will still be expected to perform the same function as before the stock transfer. In this sense we might be moving towards a more European system, where social housing is determined by its function rather than by who owns it (Oxley and Smith, 1996). The Blair government clearly intends that social rents should remain below market levels. Indeed, its proposal to restructure social rents so that they are more comparable across all social landlords is a further indication of this Europeanisation. We may therefore be moving to a position where it is less important who owns the stock than who can access and afford it. In this sense, whether it is owned by a local authority, a housing association or a private company does not much matter.

Of course, others regard it as important that council housing is preserved. One could argue that local housing assets should remain under local political control. Councillors can be held to account in ways that housing association management boards cannot. However, if my argument about the centralisation of political control in housing has any merit, any local control by councillors is largely illusory. Moreover, the 2000 green paper does not envisage altering the strategic enabling function of a local authority. Indeed, the government intends rather to strengthen it.

What is clear is that the 2000 green paper does not see the current pattern of ownership and control as an option. Change of one sort or another is inevitable. Quite what form that change will take is another question.

Is the current system of housing benefit sustainable?

The 2000 green paper was intended to consider three areas of crucial importance in housing policy, namely, rents, choice in allocations and the reform of housing benefit. The first two issues are dealt with in detail and with a degree of enthusiasm, indicating that significant change is likely to occur.

However, despite being dealt with in detail in the green paper, housing benefit reform is indefinitely postponed. As we saw in Chapter 8, the argument given for postponing reform is that the proposals on choice and rents need to be implemented first. What we need to consider here is whether the government's position is a sustainable one.

The green paper does make several limited proposals to streamline the administration of housing benefit and to deal with fraud. However, these proposals are likely to be lost in the complexity of the benefit system. Indeed, it is its very complexity that allows fraud to be undertaken so readily. Yet proposals to simplify the system by flat-rate payments are largely dismissed in the green paper.

The green paper considers the lack of work incentives in the current system, but again proposals such as the introduction of 'shopping incentives' are considered only tentatively and the government avoids any commitment to this, or indeed, to any proposal for long-term reform. One should remember, however, that in the early years of the Blair government, ministers placed greater emphasis on the moral dimension of welfare than the financial. The welfare reform green paper (DSS, 1998) saw welfare benefits as the cost of failure and thus a new incentive structure was needed to deal with dependency and get people back into work.

The clear implication, therefore, is that having considered the various reform options, the government did not find any politically acceptable. A more charitable view would be to suggest that, having committed the housing profession to undertake choice in allocations and rent restructuring (along with resource accounting and business planning in the local authority sector), the government considered the reform of housing benefit one major change too many. Of the possible reforms the government wanted to undertake, housing benefit reform was by far the most difficult and controversial, and so it has been delayed.

But just how stable is the government's position? Whilst the cost of housing benefit has stabilised since the late 1990s, it is still due to rise slowly. There is certainly only a limited possibility of a significant reduction in the cost of housing benefit. Indeed, were there to be a recession, the cost of housing benefit would be expected to rise considerably.

On the other hand, one might argue that the biggest cause of increasing housing benefit costs has been rent increases. Therefore, so long as the government is able to control rent levels, it can cap housing benefit costs. But this fails to deal with the moral dimension of welfare dependency. Maintaining the current system means accepting that housing benefit might dissuade certain individuals from taking available jobs. This has been a priority for the government, as shown by policies such as the working families tax credit, the New Deal and the insistence that certain groups such as lone parents attend interviews with employment advisors.

The issue of dependency is essentially a political rather than a purely financial issue. The current expenditure on housing benefit, making up a little over 10 per cent of the social security budget, is affordable. It is therefore a matter of political judgement whether tackling benefit dependency is worthwhile relative to other pressing housing and welfare issues. Housing issues quite clearly are less politically significant than health and education. Likewise, housing benefit gets less political attention than do pensions. Whilst the cost of housing benefit does not rise significantly, it is likely that the government will be able to concentrate on more pressing political problems around health and education. In this sense, the current system of housing benefit is sustainable. However, this does not make it satisfactory, nor is it rational. Pragmatically, however, government has taken a chance that if it ignores housing benefit, the problem will go away.

What will be the impact of rent restructuring?

The green paper (DETR, 2000a) proposes that social housing rents need to be restructured to deal with unjustifiable differences in rent levels within local areas. As we saw in Chapter 5, the proposals involve pegging housing association rents and introducing a mechanism to converge rents in the local authority and housing association sectors.

These proposals are likely to have far-reaching consequences, particularly for housing associations, many of which have business plans predicated on real-term rent increases. Many associations will have to cut back on their development programmes in terms of either quantity or quality (and perhaps both). Some associations have suggested that they face bankruptcy as a result of the limits on rent, particularly as they may be forced into rent reductions.

The debate over rent restructuring and its potential effects on social landlords has raised a much more fundamental point about housing subsidies, namely, just whom they are intended for. The reaction of many landlords to the proposals for rent comparability was to claim that they would compromise their long-term financial viability.

However, as the chief executive of a large housing association has commented, RSLs 'are in danger of only looking at the government's ideas from [their] own perspective and not that of [their] customers'. He goes on to argue that proposals for the government to moderate the policy are 'a throw-back to the days before we became social housing businesses and took responsibility for our own destiny' (*Inside Housing*, 14 July 2000, p. 10). The suggestion therefore is that housing associations should be concerned with their tenants' rather than their own institutional interests and actually be responsible businesses instead of seeing all change as a threat and as necessitating government action to support them.

The problem, however, is that housing associations have not had to act as if they were responsible for their success or failure, nor have they been forced to focus on the needs of their tenants instead of their organisational integrity. The reason for this is their ability to capture housing benefit through direct payments and the lack of any competition from within or without the social housing sector. In this situation, housing benefit merely acts as a direct subsidy to the landlord, insulating them from risk.

This situation, of course, entirely negates the purpose of housing benefit as a personal subsidy offering a degree of choice and independence to its recipients. Housing benefit makes housing affordable, but the definition of affordability is that defined in the business plans of housing associations and not in terms of incomes or household choice.

The introduction of rent restructuring might, then, do precisely what the post-1989 system was meant to do, but didn't. It might actually introduce a proper element of risk into housing association decision-making by making it impossible to pass higher costs on to the housing benefit system by large rent increases.

I would suggest that of all the proposals in the 2000 green paper it is rent restructuring that will have the greatest impact on housing finance and on housing policy more generally. Stock transfer will take some time to build up and there needs to be some balancing between it and other mechanisms for levering private finance such as arm's-length companies and the PFI. Fundamental housing benefit reform is unlikely unless there is a major economic dislocation or a change in government.

Housing finance policy is moving into interesting times. One should remember that 'May you live in interesting times' is an old Chinese curse wishing ill on one's enemies. Of course, change is never far away in housing finance policy, but the first decade of the twenty-first century is likely to be particularly full of change. As the Chinese curse implies, not all of this change will be welcome.

What we can be sure of, however, is that there will be many unforeseen developments and new complexities that politicians and experts did not expect. In this sense the future promises to be genuinely interesting, as we struggle to understand just what is going on with housing finance.

Summary

In this chapter I have looked at three key questions for the future of housing finance policy, namely:

- Is there a future for council housing in the light of proposals for increased stock transfer?
- Is the current system of housing benefit sustainable?
- What will be the impact of rent restructuring on housing associations?

Further reading

Keeping abreast of current issues is important in such a fast-moving area as housing finance. The best starting points are magazines such as *Housing*, *Housing Today*, *Inside Housing* and *Roof* that consider housing issues as they are developing. Another key source for the breaking issues is government websites, particularly those of the DETR (www.detr.gov.uk) and DSS (www.dss.gov.uk). Alternatively, you could wait for the second edition of this book!

# Glossary

Below are a number of terms that are used throughout the book. I have attempted to give brief and clear definitions of these terms and have made additional comments where relevant.

Annual Capital Guideline (ACG) The amount of capital expenditure each local authority is deemed by government to need to spend in a particular year. The ACG consists of capital receipts, borrowing and grants for private-sector work.

Arm's-length companies It was proposed in the 2000 green paper (DETR, 2000a) to establish autonomous arm's-length companies to manage local authority-owned housing, with the best-performing authorities given extra scope to borrow from the private sector. Only the best-performing local authorities are to be allowed to establish these companies.

Basic credit approvals (BCAs) The amount of debt a local authority can incur in any one year. BCAs are allocated by the Department of the Environment, Transport and the Regions, and are backed by the Treasury. Hence they count as public spending, even though BCAs are permission to incur debt, and not grants.

Best Value Introduced by the Labour government that came to power in 1997; it replaced Compulsory Competitive Tendering. Instead of putting services out to tender, local authorities are to measure their performance against a series of performance indicators and local good practice to ensure that they achieve continual improvement in service delivery.

Business planning The process whereby each local authority submits a business plan outlining its long-term plans (up to thirty years) for the use and enhancing of its assets (i.e. its housing stock).

Capital The form of finance that enhances the asset value of the housing stock. It therefore deals with the acquisition and development of land, buildings, plant and machinery. It also covers those repairs and improvements funded through borrowing and capital grants.

Capital receipts Income received from the sale of houses and land. Local authorities are able to use only a proportion of their receipts in any one year (25 per cent of house sales and 50 per cent for land sales). Accumulated balances are allocated according to the Capital receipts initiative, which should have reallocated all accumulated receipts by 2002 (see **Receipts taken into account**).

Compulsory Competitive Tendering (CCT) The system whereby local authorities had to put their services out to tender and generally accept the cheapest contractor. The aim was to increase efficiency by market-testing services. CCT was replaced by Best Value in 1999.

Department of the Environment, Transport and the Regions (DETR) The government department that deals primarily with housing and local government in England. Prior to 1997 it was known as the Department of the Environment (DoE).

Equity withdrawal The practice where a portion of the asset value of a house is used for another purpose. This is possible because of the increased value of the property compared to the size of the initial mortgage loan to fund its purchase.

Generalised Needs Index (GNI) The means used to determine the allocation of resources to local authorities. The GNI brings together a series of indicators such as incomes, land values, unemployment and homelessness to determine the relative need of each region and local authority for resources.

Grant Redemption Fund (GRF) The mechanism in operation until 1989 to claw back surpluses on housing association housing action grant-funded schemes. Surpluses could be used to fund major repairs, used to offset deficits on other schemes or be taken back by the Housing Corporation and recirculated via the Approved Development Programme. It was replaced by the Rent Surplus Fund.

Grant stretch The process of limiting the call on social housing grant in housing association development by using reserves or local authority funds or land. The prevailing grant rate serves as the maximum allowable public funding for a scheme. Thus local authority resources used in development have to be valued and this reduces the grant level accordingly.

Hostel Deficit Grant (HDG) The mechanism used between 1974 and 1989 to fund loss-making hostel schemes developed by housing associations. It was replaced in 1989 by the Transitional Special Needs Management Allowance. This was replaced in turn by Supported housing management grant. Also see **Supporting People**.

Housing association grant (HAG) Until 1996, the grant paid to housing associations to allow them to build. Prior to 1989 the level of grant was set only after the completion of the scheme (hence *residual* or *deficit* HAG). After 1989 HAG was *predetermined* and therefore grant rate was fixed at the start of development. HAG was replaced by social housing grant in 1996.

Housing benefit The means-tested subsidy paid to low-income households to help them afford rented housing.

Housing Corporation The organisation that funds, regulates, monitors and promotes housing associations and other registered social landlords. It is funded by government and operates in line with government policy, but has some operational independence.

Housing Inspectorate The government-appointed body charged with monitoring the performance of local authorities and registered social landlords. It inspects and grades aspects of the landlord function and issues public reports.

Housing investment programme (HIP) Annual bid by a local authority outlining the priorities for investment for the financial year. Effectively this is a bid for annual capital spending.

Housing Needs Index (HNI) The means used to determine the allocation of resources to the Housing Corporation's regional offices, which then allocate resources to housing associations on the basis of more localised housing needs indices. The HNI brings together a series of indicators such as incomes, land values, unemployment and homelessness to determine the relative need of each region and local authority area for resources.

Housing repairs account Under resource accounting, the Department of the Environment, Transport and the Regions advises that the major repairs allowance and any other contribution to major repairs be transferred to a housing repairs account, where expenditure in this area would be accounted for.

Housing revenue account (HRA) The income and expenditure account maintained by each local authority for its own housing stock.

Large-scale voluntary transfer (LSVT) The practice of transferring all or a significant proportion of a local authority's housing stock to a housing association or other registered social landlord. LSVT became a serious development in 1990 after the introduction of the Local Government and Housing Act 1989, which tightened the controls on expenditure.

Local reference rents (LRRs) The system where housing benefit payments are restricted to what is a reasonable rent for that area and what it is reasonable for each particular household to expect to reside in. Thus the system aims to ensure that households do not occupy dwellings that are too expensive or too large for their needs.

Major repairs allowance (MRA) An annual allowance for each local authority to spend on major repairs and maintenance. As from 2001, this involves the reallocation of basic credit approvals and is paid into the housing revenue account.

Means testing The targeting of benefits onto the most needy, so that the amount of benefit (e.g. housing benefit) paid is determined by income and circumstances. Means-tested benefits are the opposite of universal benefits, such as child benefit, which are paid regardless of income.

Mortgage interest tax relief (MITR) The system where all taxpayers received a proportion of the tax repaid to offset the cost of mortgage interest. Acted as a subsidy to owner occupiers. Abolished in 2000.

Notional housing revenue account The mechanism used by the Department of the Environment, Transport and the Regions to determine the level of subsidy paid to a local authority. Made up of reckonable income and expenditure (i.e. what the local authority 'ought' to spend); the difference between these two amounts determines the level of subsidy. This level of subsidy is paid regardless of the actual level of income and expenditure.

Private Finance Initiative (PFI) A mechanism for funding public-sector capital projects. The public body engages a private contractor to build and manage the project for a set period of time in return for an annual fee. Hence capital projects are funded out of revenue income, often with additional government resources. Pathfinder projects were established by a number of local authorities in 2000 to see if the PFI can work for council housing.

Public Works Loans Board (PWLB) A Treasury-backed body that lends money to local authorities. The rate of interest is determined by the Treasury and is normally below market rates. The purpose of the board is to make borrowing cheaper, which it does by borrowing large sums and then making smaller loans to local authorities.

Receipts taken into account (RTIAs) The amount of usable capital receipts that the Department of the Environment, Transport and the Regions calculates a local authority will have for use in any financial year. RTIAs are used to offset entitlement to basic credit approvals.

Registered social landlord (RSL) Landlords who are eligible to receive social housing grant from the Housing Corporation, having registered and met the corporation's criteria. The overwhelming majority of RSLs are housing associations.

Rent capping The policy since 1996 whereby rent rebate (housing benefit) subsidy is restricted to the rent guideline level rather than the actual rents charged.

Rent control Where landlords are not permitted to increase rents above a ceiling. Statutory (i.e. enforced by legislation) rent controls were introduced in 1915 and existed largely until 1989. Administrative measures such as rent capping and local reference rents are a form of administrative rent control.

Rent guideline The annual rent increase (or decrease) that government expects each local authority to apply. The government assumes the guideline is met and sets HRA subsidy accordingly. The system from 2001 is subsumed into rent restructuring.

Rent pooling The practice of setting rents according to the attributes of properties rather than according to actual costs. Thus rents on older properties are higher than are actually needed to manage and maintain them, whilst rents on newer stock are lower.

Rent restructuring The policy, from 2002, of setting target rents for each unit of social housing based on a formula of 70 per cent local incomes and 30 per cent property values. The aim is to achieve these target rents within a ten-year period, although no rent will change by more than £2 per week. In addition, rent increases for housing associations are to be restricted to inflation plus 0.5 per cent.

Rent Surplus Fund (RSF) The mechanism used to capture rent surpluses (of reckonable income over reckonable expenditure) on deficit housing action grant-funded schemes. Associations must put inflation-linked increases into the RSF. The fund can be used only to fund major repairs or to build up reserves.

Resource accounting Introduced into local authority housing revenue finance in 2001. Based on the use that a local authority's assets are put to rather than the historic cost of their formation. Local authorities are obliged to make a 6 per cent capital charge against their housing revenue account. The aim of resource accounting is to make authorities more businesslike in their operation and more aware of their investment needs. It is intended to place a much higher priority on major repairs and maintenance.

Revenue Revenue is that finance needed to manage the day-to-day running costs of the housing service. It therefore covers staff salaries, management and maintenance, and other administrative costs.

Revenue deficit grant (RDG) A grant given to housing associations between 1974 and 1989 to assist in the funding of loss-making schemes. The grant was deemed necessary because associations could not set their own rents. RDG was abolished in 1989.

Ring fencing The Local Government and Housing Act 1989 prevented local authorities from passing funds between their housing revenue account and general fund. This meant that local authorities were not able to use rents to subsidise other council services such as education, or use the council tax (or rates as it then was) to fund council housing and keep rents artificially low.

Shopping incentives These are aimed at introducing some incentive for housing benefit recipients to choose cheaper housing. Instead of housing benefit being paid according to actual rent levels, it would be restricted to a set proportion of the actual rent (say 80 per cent). The difference would be met from income support, which would be uprated accordingly. The aim is to make rent levels important to both landlords and tenants and to offer benefit recipients some choice. Shopping incentives were mentioned favourably in the 2000 housing green paper, but no action has been taken to implement them.

Single capital pot From 2001, instead of local authorities receiving separate credit approvals for housing, education, transport, social services and other services, they are to be put all together into one capital expenditure fund. This will allow more discretion in the mix of spending according to local priorities.

Single room rent (SRR) regulation This restricts the amount of benefit paid to single persons under 25 to that of shared accommodation in the local area. The regulation applies only to the private rented sector.

Social housing grant (SHG) The grant paid to housing associations and other registered social landlords by the Housing Corporation to subsidise the cost of developing new dwellings. Until 1996 was known as housing association grant. The level of SHG is determined by local grant rates and is also dependent on the type of scheme.

Special needs management allowance The mechanism introduced in 1989 to help fund loss-making special needs projects managed by housing associations. This allowance was claimable only for schemes built using mixed funding.

Specified capital grants Annual grants made by government to local authorities, which form part of the Annual Capital Guideline but may only be used to fund private-sector activity, such as improvement grants to owner occupiers.

Subsidy An explicit or implicit flow of funds initiated by government activity, which reduces the relative cost of housing.

Supplementary credit approvals (SCAs) Additional permissions to borrow and incur debt over and above basic credit approvals. They can be granted at any time in the financial year and are usually used for government initiatives such as regeneration projects.

Supported housing management grant (SHMG) A grant made in order to assist housing associations in funding supported housing schemes. In 2003, SHMG is to be incorporated into the Supporting People mechanism.

Supporting People An attempt to co-ordinate the funding of supported housing by bringing together the disparate forms of funding. From 2003, each local authority will control funds for supported housing in its area. The fund will bring together supported housing management grant, probation accommodation grant and the element of housing benefit and support services (such as wardens) that is paid for through income support.

Tax expenditures The accounting term used for government subsidies, such as mortgage interest tax relief, which reduce the amount of money available to government and make an activity cheaper than it otherwise would be. They thus have the same effect as a direct subsidy.

Appendix: Learning activity answers

The learning activities distributed throughout the text are intended to reinforce certain key issues and to aid reflection on these issues. They might also assist those teaching housing finance. Some of the learning activities will take only a few minutes to complete, whilst others will take several hours and might be useful as essay questions or as the basis for an assignment. Other learning activities might be used as the stepping-off points for discussions.

I have included suggested answers to the learning activities below. Some are precise answers, whilst others are possible answers or the sorts of issues that might be raised. In the latter cases, the answers below are not the only answers, and therefore if you have come up with some other list then this is not to say you are wrong. I hope that it won't indicate that I am, either.

ACTIVITY 2.1: Consider why the state intervenes in housing markets. What are the main ways in which it intervenes?

The state intervenes to correct market failures, ensure or improve standards, meet certain political and economic goals, redistribute from rich to poor, and to attain uniformity across the country. The main ways in which it intervenes are via legislation, regulation, monitoring and funding.

ACTIVITY 2.2: List those housing subsidies that either you have received or you currently do receive.

The possible subsidies are mortgage interest tax relief and other tax reliefs, housing benefit, local authority or housing association tenancies (subsidised rent), improvement grants, shared ownership, low-cost home ownership and the cash incentive scheme.

ACTIVITY 2.3: What are the effects on housing organisations of the shift from object to subject subsidies? Who has benefited from this shift?

The effects of moving towards subject subsidies include lower direct subsidies, a greater reliance on rents and housing benefit, reduced or no development of new dwellings and a general commercialisation because of the need to maximise income. The main beneficiaries of this change are private lenders, who receive a reasonable rate of return from lending to social landlords, who receive less direct subsidy. In theory, if not in practice, tenants have greater choice of landlord if they, rather than landlords, receive the subsidy.

ACTIVITY 2.4: Discuss why in Britain we maintain elements of both object and subject subsidies.

The main reason is that we do not have a planned system, but rather one that has developed gradually over time. Certain elements are changed, but there is seldom a root-and-branch overhaul of the system. Another reason is that there are strong vested interests in and attachments to certain parts of the system, particularly council housing.

ACTIVITY 3.1: List the benefits to tenants of government intervention into housing. Why was intervention resisted by landlords?

Possible benefits are cheaper rents, higher standards, standard tenancy arrangements across the country allowing for mobility, protection from arbitrary eviction and harassment, and improvements in health as a result of higher standards. Landlords resisted the intervention on grounds of the increased costs they incurred and on the liberal principle that government had no right to intervene in private property.

ACTIVITY 3.2: Give three examples of how changes to housing subsidies have had a major effect on the type of housing provided.

Possible examples include rent control, capital subsidies to local authorities, higher subsidy for high-rise buildings, subsidies for slum clearance, housing association grant, mortgage interest tax relief, improvement grants, the Business Expansion Scheme.

ACTIVITY 4.1: Make a list, in order of importance, of the activities of a local authority housing department. Where does the money come from?

It is a matter of judgement as to what order of importance you put the list in, but it should consist of managing dwellings, allocations, rent collection, dealing with arrears, void inspections, maintenance, major repairs, homelessness, enabling other social landlords and housing advice. The money comes from rents and government subsidy.

ACTIVITY 4.2: What are the advantages of central control of housing?

Possible advantages are ensuring uniformity across the country, attaining high standards, value for money and efficiency, proper use and control of public funds, co-ordination with other services such as health and social services, and allowing for concerted national strategies on important issues such as homelessness and rough sleeping.

ACTIVITY 4.3: Give reasons why the following are preferably determined locally rather than by centrally determined policy:

- **Rent levels**: Average incomes differ according to locality; local politicians may see poverty as a key local issue.
- **Maintenance expenditure**: Particular local problems might mean higher expenditure, such as high rise, or a higher proportion of old stock.
- **Management budgets**: High arrears and voids; decentralisation; rural LAs might have property dispersed across a wide area.
- **Development funding**: High-demand areas will have a shortage of housing; older stock will need higher major repairs spending.

ACTIVITY 4.4: Using the formula ACG – SCG – RTIA = BCA, calculate the amount of BCAs where:

ACG = £5 million
SCG = £0.5 million
RTIA = £1.75 million

£5 million – £0.5 million – £1.75 million = £2.75 million. Therefore BCAs are £2.75 million.

ACTIVITY 4.5: Consider what capital finance could be used for, now that local authorities are not building new dwellings.

The possibilities are major repairs (this will be the majority of expenditure with the introduction of the major repairs allowance in 2001) and funding other social landlords to meet housing need in the local area.

ACTIVITY 4.6: Referring back to Table 4.2, calculate the amount of subsidy where:

Reckonable income	**= £17.5 million**
Reckonable expenditure	**= £14.5 million**
Rent rebates	**= £18 million**

Subtracting expenditure (£14.5 million) from income (£17.5 million) gives a negative subsidy entitlement (surplus) of £3 million. This surplus should be taken away from rent rebate subsidy (£18 million), leaving a total subsidy of £15 million. Total income (reckonable income plus subsidy) and expenditure (reckonable expenditure plus rent rebates) will balance at £32.5 million.

ACTIVITY 4.7: List the reasons why rents rose so much between 1989 and 1996. How could this have been avoided?

Rent increases were due to a combination of reducing subsidies and higher management and maintenance expenditure. Increases could have been avoided by providing more subsidy, by lower spending or by means of tighter central government control.

ACTIVITY 5.1: List the main differences between housing associations and local authorities.

Important differences include the fact that local authorities are part of the state, whilst associations are private bodies; associations receive grants to develop but councils must obtain loans; housing associations can borrow without Treasury backing, but councils cannot; local authorities tend to be much larger and are restricted to a particular locality, whilst associations can be active regionally or nationally; local authorities are under political control by elected councillors, whilst associations are managed by self-appointed volunteers; associations are operating voluntarily, whilst local authorities have a statutory role.

ACTIVITY 5.2: What are the advantages of housing associations and local authorities co-ordinating development together?

Associations have access to development funding, but local authorities have the statutory duty to meet housing need in their area; local authority grants or land may aid grant stretch and make a scheme viable; co-operation may help ease particular problems such as homelessness; competition between social landlords might lead to a duplication of outputs and waste of resources.

ACTIVITY 5.3: Discuss whether it matters if housing associations use public or private funding as long as new social housing is built.

The important issue here is affordability as higher levels of private finance lead to higher rents. But this could be offset by housing benefit rather than by social housing grant. Some would argue that this would be a more targeted form of assistance. On the other hand, higher levels of grant might increase the quality of the stock built. In political terms it might matter greatly, in that politicians are accountable for their policies but bankers are not!

ACTIVITY 5.4: Consider the reasons why housing association rents might be higher than local authority rents.

Housing association rents are higher because of the pressures of private finance and the need to build up reserves. But also, since the 1990s, associations have been less rigidly controlled than local authorities. Also, their rents have always tended to be higher.

ACTIVITY 6.1: What are the words which you most associate with the private sector?

Obviously what words you choose are a personal thing, but I would guess they are more likely to be derogatory and relate to issues of poor quality and decline.

ACTIVITY 6.2: What are the attractions of the private rented sector? Who might the tenure appeal to now?

Its attractions are cheapness; the fact that access is not by a waiting list but by ability to pay the rent; it allows mobility and flexibility in terms of sharing with others. The sector also contains within it a huge diversity of property from the cheap bedsit to luxury flats in, say, Chelsea. The tenure would appeal to mobile groups such as young single people and students, recent immigrants and those groups ineligible for social housing, but who might want to or be able to buy.

ACTIVITY 6.3: Compare the financial subsidies offered to the private rented sector with those offered to social housing. Give reasons for the differential treatment between the two rented sectors.

The basic difference is that subsidies are more significant for social housing and take the form of grants or direct subsidies such as housing revenue account subsidy and social housing grant. Private landlords receive only indirect subsidy via housing benefit, but then so do social landlords.

The reason for differential treatment is essentially that social landlords were established *by subsidy*. Private landlords have been subsidised neither by Labour (because they operate on a for-profit basis instead of according to need) nor by the Conservatives (because of the Conservatives' belief in not interfering in property rights). More recently the private rented sector has been neglected because it is not large enough to be politically significant.

ACTIVITY 6.4: What is the future role of the private rented sector?

Obviously any answer is conjecture, but I would think the future will not be very different from what happened in the 1990s. The sector will stay around 10–12 per cent of the total, with no great increase or decline, unless there is a change in policy on issues such as housing benefit or tenancy regulations.

ACTIVITY 7.1: Discuss why owner occupation is so popular in the UK.

The reasons have to do with government subsidies that have encouraged it and, along with supportive political rhetoric, have created a favourable climate for the tenure. But the tenure does genuinely encourage choice and independence in a way that renting never can. Therefore politicians have been pushing at an open door.

ACTIVITY 7.2: List the financial advantages and disadvantages of owner occupation. Consider how the following issues affect your list:

- income
- gender
- age
- single or joint purchase.

The advantages include the tax relief that one still receives; that housing is a store of wealth – it can offer financial security to one in retirement or to one's children; the fact that equity withdrawal can allow for additional expenditure. The disadvantages relate to the unknown total cost and the fact that, as it is the largest item in the household budget, changes in mortgage costs can have severe effects.

In relation to the four issues, changes in income are crucial in terms of affordability; gender is important in terms of income inequality and the attitudes of lenders; age is significant in that income will tend to fall on retirement, but it may be possible to tap into the equity of the dwelling by moving or by the various retirement leaseback schemes available; joint purchase obviously alters the cost and affordability, but might be a disadvantage if one party wants to sell and the other doesn't. Also, in the latter case, any capital gain is shared.

ACTIVITY 7.3: Explain the key differences between subsidies to owner occupation and those to rented housing. What accounts for the differential treatment?

The main difference is that subsidies to owner occupation have not been targeted, and still largely remain untargeted. Subsidies to renting are based on need and are increasingly means tested. The other difference is that subsidies to owner occupation are in the form of tax expenditures, allowing taxpayers to keep more of their own money. The difference has arisen because of the historic purpose of social housing, which is to meet housing need, and subsidies to social housing have thus been targeted at specific organisations and client groups. One should also not ignore the political consequences of relating tax relief to independence and personal responsibility.

ACTIVITY 8.1: Explain why we need a housing benefit system.

The main reason is to make housing affordable for those on a low income. The purpose of a benefit system should be to ensure that the sole criterion for access to good-quality housing is need and not ability to pay. A comprehensive benefit system makes housing in all tenures affordable, even the private rented sector, which has not received object subsidies to make rents cheaper.

ACTIVITY 8.2: Clearly outline the differences in the operation of housing benefit between the different tenures.

Owner occupiers have no access to housing benefit, which is reserved for renters. Private renters face restrictions to their eligibility in the form of the local reference rent (LRR) and single room rent (SRR). Housing association tenants might face the LRR, but most do not and therefore are relatively free of restrictions. Local authority tenants likewise are free of restrictions. However, rent rebate subsidy in the council sector is restricted.

ACTIVITY 8.3: Why have landlords become so dependent on housing benefit? Is this a problem of the housing benefit system, or due to other factors such as the withdrawal of object subsidies?

Landlords have become dependent for two reasons: the increasing number of tenants in receipt of benefit and the reduction in object subsidies such as housing revenue account subsidy and social housing grant. As a result, they are more dependent on rents, which have risen, and housing benefit is a secure way of guaranteeing rent payments. The problem is therefore partly due to the reduction in object subsidies, but also partly due to the way the benefit system works, in that eligible tenants can have all their rent paid.

ACTIVITY 8.4: Who has most to benefit from the reform of housing benefit?

This, of course, largely depends on the nature of the reform. The government might benefit if it led to a reduction in cost. Tenants might benefit if the system were made more generous, say if tapers were reduced. Tenants might also benefit in the long run if payments were made to them instead of the landlord and thus they became more independent of their landlords. Society as a whole would benefit from there being fewer people on benefit, but not if it meant more people facing extreme poverty.

ACTIVITY 9.1: List the important financial elements in the housing green paper *Quality and Choice: A Decent Home for All* **(DETR, 2000a).**

The main financial elements are rent restructuring, reform of housing benefit, increasing stock transfer and the Starter Home Initiative.

ACTIVITY 9.2: Discuss why fundamental change in housing policy is so difficult to achieve.

Fundamental change will be difficult if there is no consensus on the nature or scale of current problems. Also, it is impossible to stop current provision, scrap the current structures and start from scratch. Reforms can only take place whilst the current system remains in operation and thus any reform will be piecemeal. A further reason is that housing systems are so complex that no one can hope fully to understand all aspects of them. One should also be aware that there are vested interests that will fight against certain changes which are perceived to be detrimental to them.

ACTIVITY 9.3: List what you consider to be the most important housing finance policies of the past twenty years.

Obviously, this is a matter of judgement, but I would suggest that the introduction of the right to buy, the use of private finance in housing association development, the abolition of rent controls and the shift from object to subject subsidies should all rank highly.

ACTIVITY 10.1: What do you consider to be the most important housing finance issues over the next decade? Pick out at least three key issues and give reasons why you think they will be so important.

Again this is a matter of judgement, but I have suggested three issues in Chapter 10: stock transfer, housing benefit and rent restructuring. I see these as being important because they potentially will change both the structures and the culture of housing.

Bibliography

Albon, R. and Stafford, D. (1987): *Rent Control*, London, Croom Helm.

Armstrong, H (1999a): 'Let's go green', *Inside Housing*, 19 March 1999.

—— (1999b): 'A new vision for housing in England', in Brown, T. (ed.), *Stakeholder Housing: A Third Way*, London, Pluto, pp. 122–32.

Ball, M. (1983): *Housing and Economic Power: The Political Economy of Owner Occupation*, London, Methuen.

Barlow, J. and Duncan, S. (1994): *Success and Failure in Housing Provision*, Oxford, Pergamon.

Bevan, M., Kemp, P. and Rhodes, D. (1995): *Private Landlords and Housing Benefit*, York, Centre for Housing Policy.

Blair, T. (1998): *The Third Way: New Politics for the New Century*, London, Fabian Society.

Blake, J. (1998): 'Question time', *Roof*, vol. 23, no. 5, September/October 1998, pp. 19–21.

Boddy, M. (1992): 'From mutual interests to market forces', in Grant, C. (ed.), *Built to Last? Reflections on British Housing Policy*, London, Roof, pp. 40–9.

Brown, T. (ed.) (1999a): *Stakeholder Housing: A Third Way*, London, Pluto.

—— (1999b): 'The Third Way', in Brown, T. (ed.), *Stakeholder Housing: A Third Way*, London, Pluto, pp. 8–31.

Burnett, J. (1986): *A Social History of Housing, 1815–1985*, London, Methuen.

Chaplin, R., Jones, M., Martin, S., Pryke, M., Royce, C., Whitehead, C. and Yang, J. (1995): *Rents and Risks: Investing in Housing Associations*, York, Joseph Rowntree Foundation.

Chartered Institute of Public Finance and Accountancy (undated): *Manual of Housing Finance*, London, CIPFA.

Cole, I. and Furbey, R. (1994): *The Eclipse of Council Housing*, London, Routledge.

Coleman, D. (1992): 'The 1987 housing policy: an enduring reform?', in Birchall, J. (ed.): *Housing Policy in the 1990s*, London, Routledge, pp. 113–39.

Cope, H. (1999): *Housing Associations: Policy and Practice*, second edition, Basingstoke, Macmillan.

Crook, A. and Kemp, P. (1996): 'The revival of private rented housing in Britain', *Housing Studies*, vol. 11, no. 1, pp. 51–68.

Damer, S. (1992): 'Striking out on Red Clyde', in Grant, C. (ed.), *Built to Last? Reflections on British Housing Policy*, London, Roof, pp. 35–9.

Daunton, M. (1987): *A Property Owning Democracy?*, London, Faber.

Department of the Environment (DoE) (1987): *Housing: The Government's Proposals*, London, HMSO.

—— (1995): *Our Future Homes: Opportunity, Choice and Responsibility*, London, HMSO.

Department of the Environment, Transport and the Regions (DETR) (1998): *Modernising Local Government: Capital Finance*, London, The Stationery Office.

—— (1999): *Housing Benefit and Private Landlords*, London, DETR.

—— (2000a): *Quality and Choice: A Decent Home for All*, London, DETR/DSS.

—— (2000b): *Modernising Local Government Finance: A Green Paper*, London, DETR.

—— (2000c): *Quality and Choice: A Decent Home for All – The Way Forward for Housing*, London, DETR.

—— (2000d): *Guide to Social Rent Reforms*, London, DETR.

—— (2000e): *Assessing the Impact of Housing Green Paper Rent Reform Policies on Individual Registered Social Landlords*, London, DETR.

Department of Social Security (DSS) (1997): *Social Security Support for Housing Costs*, Welfare Reform focus file 5, London, DSS.

—— (1998): *New Ambitions for our Country: A New Contract for Welfare*, London, The Stationery Office.

Devigne, R. (1994): *Recasting Conservatism: Oakeshott, Strauss, and the Response to Postmodernism*, New Haven, Yale University Press.

Field, F. (1996): *Stakeholder Welfare*, London, Institute of Economic Affairs.

Forrest, R., Murie, A. and Williams, P. (1990): *Home Ownership: Differentiation and Fragmentation*, London, Hyman.

Gamble, A. (1988): *The Free Economy and the Strong State: The Politics of Thatcherism*, Basingstoke, Macmillan.

Garnett, D. (2000): *Housing Finance*, Coventry, Chartered Institute of Housing.

Gauldie, E. (1974): *Cruel Habitations*, London, Allen & Unwin.

Gibb, K., Munro, M. and Satsangi, M. (1999): *Housing Finance in the UK: An Introduction*, second edition, Basingstoke, Macmillan.

Green, D. (1993): *Reinventing Civil Society*, London, Institute of Economic Affairs.

Hayek, F. (1960): *The Constitution of Liberty*, London, Routledge & Kegan Paul.

Hills, J. (1991): *Unravelling Housing Finance: Subsidies, Benefits and Taxation*, Oxford, Clarendon.

—— (1997): *The Future of Welfare: A Guide to the Debate*, second revised edition, York, Joseph Rowntree Foundation.

Hitchens, P. (1999): *The Abolition of Britain: From Lady Chatterley to Tony Blair*, London, Quartet Books.

Holmans, A. (1987): *Housing Policy in Britain: A History*, London, Croom Helm.

Jenkins, S. (1995): *Accountable to None: The Tory Nationalization of Britain*, London, Hamish Hamilton.

Kemp, P. (1997): *A Comparative Study of Housing Allowances*, London, HMSO.

—— (1998): *Housing Benefit: Time for Reform*, York, Joseph Rowntree Foundation.

—— (2000): *'Shopping Incentives' and Housing Benefit Reform*, York, Joseph Rowntree Foundation/Chartered Institute of Housing.

King, P. (1996): *The Limits of Housing Policy: A Philosophical Investigation*, London, Middlesex University Press.

—— (1997): 'Constructivism, individual action and housing finance: an individualist critique of approaches to housing finance', *Netherlands Journal of Housing and the Built Environment*, vol. 12, no. 3, pp. 307–23.

—— (1998): *Housing, Individuals and the State: The Morality of Government Intervention*, London, Routledge.

—— (1999): 'The reform of housing benefit', *Economic Affairs*, vol. 19, no. 3, pp. 9–13.

—— (2000): *Housing Benefit: What the Government Ought to Do, but Won't*, London, Adam Smith Institute.

King, P. and Oxley, M. (2000): *Housing: Who Decides?*, Basingstoke, Macmillan.

Levine, D. (1995): *Wealth and Freedom: An Introduction to Political Economy*, Cambridge, Cambridge University Press.

MacCormick, N. (1993): 'Constitutionalism and democracy', in Bellamy, R. (ed.), *Theories and Concepts of Politics*, Manchester, Manchester University Press, pp. 124–47.

McCrone, G. and Stephens, M. (1995): *Housing Policy in Britain and Europe*, London, UCL Press.

Malpass, P. (1990): *Reshaping Housing Policy: Subsidies, Rents and Residualisation*, London, Routledge.

—— (2000): *Housing Associations and Housing Policy: A Historical Perspective*, Basingstoke, Macmillan.

Malpass, P. and Aughton, H. (1999): *Housing Finance: A Basic Guide*, fifth edition, London, Shelter.

Malpass, P. and Murie, A. (1999): *Housing Policy and Practice*, fifth edition, Basingstoke, Macmillan.

Malpass, P., Warburton, M., Bramley, G. and Smart, G. (1993): *Housing Policy in Action: The New Financial Regime for Council Housing*, Bristol, Saus.

Marsland, D. (1996): *Welfare or Welfare State? Contradictions and Dilemmas in Social Policy*, Basingstoke, Macmillan.

Murray, C. (1996): *Charles Murray and the Underclass: The Developing Debate*, London, Institute of Economic Affairs.

Oxley, M. (2000): 'Governments and social welfare', in King, P. and Oxley, M. (eds), *Housing: Who Decides?*, Basingstoke, Macmillan, pp. 70–124.

Oxley, M. and Smith, J. (1996): *Housing Policy and Rented Housing in Europe*, London, Spon.

Page, D. (1993): *Building for Communities*, York, Joseph Rowntree Foundation.

Power, A. (1987): *Property before People: The Management of Twentieth Century Council Housing*, Hemel Hempstead, Allen & Unwin.

—— (1993): *From Hovels to Highrise: State Housing in Europe since 1850*, London, Routledge.

Saunders, P. (1990): *A Nation of Home Owners*, London, Allen & Unwin.

Skidelsky, R. (1996): 'Welfare without the state', *Prospect*, vol. 4, January, pp. 38–43.

Smith, J. (1997): *What Determines Housing Investment?*, Delft, Delft University Press.

Somerville, P. and Knowles, A. (1991): 'The difference tenure makes', *Housing Studies*, vol. 6, no. 2, pp. 112–30.

Wilcox, S. (1997): *Replacing Housing Benefit with Housing Credit*, Coventry, Chartered Institute of Housing.

—— (1999): *Housing Finance Review, 1999/2000*, York, Joseph Rowntree Foundation.

—— (2000): *Housing Finance Review, 2000/2001*, York, Joseph Rowntree Foundation.

Williams, H. (1998): *Guilty Men: Conservative Decline and Fall, 1992–1997*, London, Aurum Press.

Wood, J. and Harvey, J. (1999): 'A financial perspective', in Brown, T. (ed.), *Stakeholder Housing: A Third Way*, London, Pluto, pp. 225–34.

Zebedee, J. and Ward, M. (2000): *Guide to Housing Benefit and Council Tax Benefit, 2000–2001*, London, Shelter/Chartered Institute of Housing.

Index